This book is a must-read if you…

- are ready to master your mindset and build the resilience needed to navigate life's challenges.
- are a corporate leader seeking innovative strategies to create a wellness-driven, high-performance culture within your organisation.
- value mental wellness as a cornerstone of success and want to empower your team or organisation to thrive under pressure.
- believe in the power of growth and transformation and want a clear roadmap to embrace change and turn adversity into opportunity.
- aspire to live abundantly, aligning your life or leadership with your values, vision, and purpose.
- seek tools to cultivate emotional intelligence, self-compassion, and positive self-talk for personal and professional success.
- understand the importance of post-traumatic growth and want to rise stronger after life's storms.
- are looking to break free from a victim mentality and step into a victor mindset, no longer allowing past pain or setbacks to define you.
- want to use your lived experiences as a source of strength and empowerment, transforming challenges into opportunities for growth and leadership.
- are eager to learn about the principles of positive psychology and how they can be applied to create lasting well-being, resilience, and success.

Whether you're charting your personal path to growth or shaping the future of your organisation, *Letting Go, Keeping On, and Rising Stronger* equips you with the strategies, the wisdom, and the mindset shifts needed to thrive.

Praise for *The Path of Pearl*

"Pearl's book is an inspiring personal story and reminder of the power of resilience and perseverance in life. Pearl's story shows that challenges can be turned into learnings in the pursuit of achieving your dreams. Great read."

Jani Hirvonen
Award-Winning Leader and Athlete

....

"Trauma can impact any of us at any time, and indeed it does. From starting life in Botswana, Pearl encountered traumatic challenges from an early age and continued to do so as her life unfolded. However, despite all she had to deal with, she celebrated some wonderful personal achievements.

In *The Path of Pearl*, she keeps the reader engaged with her personal story that weaves itself into each chapter. Pearl opens up to the emotions, feelings and pain she endured on her life journey. One cannot help but admire her ability to stay resilient. Each chapter includes her generous sharing of the range of well-being and life tools she used to empower herself with to be able to keep going and follow her dreams. She resolved to survive no matter what and vowed to never give up.

Pearl is a brave and courageous lady whose story I am sure will give hope and inspiration to readers who can relate to her experiences. She shows that trauma need not hold anyone back. They can go on to achieve great things as she did, and that dreams can come true. A treasure chest of wisdom indeed that has something for everyone to dip into when life gets tough."

H.E. Dr Caroline Purvey
Author of *Feel It to Heal It*

"Pearl's story and content is relevant for every one of us. We all have something to let go of, and often the fear of letting go is stronger than the endless, yet undiscovered possibilities of that release. It is not until we let go, that we learn what is there for us. Let Pearl guide you on this journey and you cannot go wrong. She has lived it and so can you."

Dr Celine Mullins
Founder of Adaptas (adaptastraining.com)
Author of *Our Learning Brain* and *Developing Learning Habits*

....

"Reading *The Path of Pearl* has been a transformative experience for me. Pearl Letlotlo Olesitse shares her journey with raw honesty and profound insight, guiding readers through the complexities of resilience, self-belief, and personal growth. Her ability to turn adversity into opportunity is both inspiring and empowering.

The practical strategies outlined in the book – ranging from cultivating emotional intelligence to embracing a growth mindset – have equipped me with the tools I needed to navigate my own challenges. Pearl's story encourages us to reflect on our experiences and find strength in vulnerability, making this book a valuable resource for anyone seeking to enhance their mental wellness.

Whether you're a corporate leader aiming to foster a positive culture, or an individual looking for guidance in tough times, *The Path of Pearl* offers wisdom, hope, and a clear roadmap to a fulfilling life. I cannot recommend it highly enough!"

Dr Carolyn M. Rubin
Keynote Speaker, Mentor and Coach
Leadership and Healthcare Consultant

"Pearl is an absolute inspiration. She moved to Ireland and then went through cancer pretty much on her own during her final year in university and then, only a few months later, got a first-class honours degree. This was after her mum had recently passed as well. Pearl has an incredible story of resilience, courage, and how to go from victim to victor though conscious awareness and personal responsibility. You will learn a lot from her story in this book."

Doug Gordon
Award-Winning CEO, Motivational Speaker, Bestselling Author, Executive & Life Coach, Corporate Trainer, and Journalist

....

"*The Path of Pearl* is a masterpiece of wisdom, resilience, and transformation. Pearl Letlotlo Olesitse has crafted a guide that speaks to the heart of personal growth and healing, offering not just inspiration but practical tools for overcoming life's challenges.

As someone who has worked in leadership, governance, and human rights roles, I deeply resonate with the themes of perseverance, self-belief, and post-traumatic growth explored in this book. Pearl's storytelling is both intimate and universal – reminding us that adversity is not the end of the road but an invitation to rise stronger.

This book is a must-read for anyone seeking to master their mindset, embrace change, and unlock their full potential. Whether you are a leader, a professional, or an individual navigating life's complexity, *The Path of Pearl* will empower you to step into a life of abundance and purpose."

Ms Mary Izobo
International Human Rights Lawyer,
Gender Equality Advocate, and Governance Expert

"*The Path of the Pearl* is a powerful and beautifully crafted guide for anyone ready to rise stronger, lead with purpose, and live with intention. As someone deeply passionate about resilience, well-being, and transformation, I found this book to be both grounding and inspiring. It offers practical tools and profound insights for shifting from surviving to thriving – whether you're navigating personal challenges or leading others through times of change.

A must-read for those committed to cultivating emotional intelligence, embracing post-traumatic growth, and turning adversity into an opportunity for deeper alignment with your values and vision."

Julie Lewis
Explorer, Speaker, and Author of *Uncharted Waters*

....

"This is a precious book in more ways than one. It's helpful, useful, and touching.

Helpful – in its ability to ignite 'me too' moments confirming the same doesn't have to be the same to resonate.

Useful – by gifting many relevant, dexterous prompts, tools, and action steps.

Touching – as 'My Story', the personal tale from the lens of the author, weaves through the book with a compelling pull, creating a hunger for the organic narrative, chapter by chapter.

So, yes. Pearl is Precious."

Susan Furness
Content Strategist and Book Coach

The Path of Pearl

A Treasure Chest of Guidance and Wisdom

Pearl Letlotlo Olesitse

First published in Great Britain in 2025
by Book Brilliance Publishing
265A Fir Tree Road, Epsom, Surrey, KT17 3LF
+44 (0)20 8641 5090
www.bookbrilliancepublishing.com
admin@bookbrilliancepublishing.com

A CIP catalogue record for this book is available at the British Library.

ISBN 978-1-913770-98-3

Some names and identifying details have been changed to protect identities.

For my beloved mother, Maria Sedupe Olesitse (1949–2015), whose unwavering wisdom and boundless love shaped the person I am today. Though you are no longer with me, your light continues to guide my path, your words echo in my heart, and your strength inspires me every single day.

To the eighteen-year-old me, who dared to dream of this moment, even when it felt impossibly far away, this is our triumph. We did it!

And to the curious, ambitious five-year-old me, who gazed at the world with wonder and planted the seeds of a dream that would grow into this book, thank you for never losing that spark.

This book is more than words on a page; it is a celebration of resilience, transformation, and the treasures found in life's challenges.

To those who read it, may it guide you to find your own light in the dark.

CONTENTS

FOREWORD

There are some books that you just wish you'd had when your life turned upside down. *The Path of Pearl* is one such book – an offering from the soul of a woman who has chosen to transform pain into wisdom, adversity into a message, and her life into a treasure chest of hope, guidance, and strength.

Pearl Letlotlo Olesitse's work is characterised by her fierce honesty and her quiet, steadfast courage. This is not a book filled with hollow affirmations or abstract theories. Instead, it is a gentle and powerful guide, grounded in lived experience and elevated by the science of positive psychology and the transformative practices of coaching. She wears resilience like a protective cloak. Her words from a place of inner strength are carried on waves of compassion – a tone that resonates deeply with my own values as a scholar, an activist and as a woman.

As someone who has spent a lifetime in education and research, I do believe that human beings are capable of almost anything. Our minds, our bodies, and – most of all – our spirits are astonishing in their capacity to learn, grow, and recover. I have also witnessed just how fragile we humans can be. We break. We ache. We lose our way. But what sets people like Pearl apart is that they refuse to let their brokenness define them. Instead, they choose to rebuild – with kindness, with self-compassion, and with a renewed sense of purpose.

In these pages, Pearl shares her personal path through illness, grief, betrayal, and discovery of true identity. She weaves in the universal truths we all face – letting go, rediscovering self-worth, forgiving those who may never apologise, and, perhaps hardest of all, forgiving ourselves. With the vulnerability born of profound wisdom and insight, she lets us into her world, her heart, and her healing. This, to me, is the highest form of sisterhood – sharing your truth not to impress, but to empower others to rise.

This book is especially timely for leaders and change-makers in both personal and corporate spheres. As organisations seek to build inclusive and diverse cultures that are not only high-performing but also emotionally intelligent and values-driven, Pearl's insights offer a human-centred blueprint. She speaks to the power of mindset mastery and emotional awareness in creating resilience – not just in individuals, but in communities and cultures.

Her lessons – drawing on experience, and polished through reflection and study – remind us that hope is not naive. It is radical. It is essential. In a world often marred by cynicism, Pearl dares to hope. She dares to believe that love, kindness, patience, and integrity are not soft ideals but firm foundations on which to build meaningful lives and impactful leadership.

As an educator, over the years I have mentored hundreds of students and tried to be a role model for emerging leaders, and I always encourage them to find the intersection between their pain and their passion. That is where purpose lives. Pearl has found hers, and she offers it here as a gift to you.

Whether you are navigating a loss, confronting long-held limiting beliefs, or simply searching for a deeper connection with your authentic self, *The Path of Pearl* embraces you and walks beside you. This book is both balm and beacon.

In reading Pearl's journey, you may find echoes of your own. You may even feel seen, perhaps for the first time ever or in a long while. And in those moments, I invite you to pause and honour the quiet power within you – the same power that Pearl so beautifully rekindles within herself.

Thank you, Pearl, for your generosity, your honesty, and your unwavering beautiful, bright light.

May we all walk our own path of pearls – with grace, with grit, and with great compassion.

Professor Jackie Carter
University of Manchester
Author, Educator, Activist
Fellow of the Academy of Social Sciences (FAcSS)

INTRODUCTION

Success begins in the mind, and how we define it is deeply personal. For some, success means financial prosperity and career growth; for others, it is about healing, inner peace, or the ability to navigate life's storms with strength and grace. Whether you are seeking personal transformation, professional advancement, or simply a more fulfilling life, one truth remains constant: your mindset shapes your reality. Without the ability to adapt, persevere, and thrive under pressure, even the most talented individuals and organisations can struggle to reach their full potential. That's why mastering your mindset is not just beneficial, it is essential.

Drawing on principles of positive psychology, resilience, and personal mastery, *The Path of Pearl: A Treasure Chest of Guidance and Wisdom* is a deeply personal yet universally relevant guide to transformation. This book is a culmination of my life's journey, shaped by challenges, triumphs, and an unwavering determination to rise stronger. As a healthcare professional, researcher, and positive health coach, I have witnessed first-hand the power of mindset shifts in breaking free from limiting beliefs, healing from emotional wounds, and stepping into purpose. My own experiences – including navigating profound loss and surviving breast cancer in the midst of a global pandemic – have reinforced the truth that adversity is not the end of the road, it is often the beginning of something greater. Through this book, I share not only my own insights but also proven, actionable strategies to help you overcome obstacles, embrace change, and build a life of confidence, resilience, and abundance.

This journey is divided into nine transformative sections, each guiding you through a different stage of personal growth and self-mastery:

- **Letting Go – Embracing the Power of Release:** Before we can grow, we must first release what no longer serves us. This section helps you break free from past narratives, fears, and the illusion of control, teaching you to trust the process and make space for new beginnings.
- **Keep On Keeping On – Building Inner Strength:** Resilience is not about avoiding hardship but about learning how to rise after a fall. You will explore the importance of renewal, self-reflection, and the courage to start over with clarity and wisdom.
- **Hope – The Foundation of Growth:** Hope is the driving force that keeps us moving forward. This chapter delves into aligning with your values, cultivating a growth mindset, and harnessing the transformative power of kindness, both to yourself and others.
- **Grief – Healing and Self-Compassion:** Loss is an inevitable part of life, but suffering does not have to be. You will gain insights into navigating grief with grace, understanding the stages of loss, and applying mindfulness and self-compassion to your healing journey.
- **Patience and Perseverance – Strengthening Your Resilience:** True success takes time. This chapter

teaches you how to develop patience, endure challenges without losing yourself, and stay committed to long-term growth in a fast-paced world.

- **Self-Belief – The Key to Empowerment:** Your greatest power lies in believing in yourself. Learn how to communicate effectively, own your voice, and lead with confidence, turning self-doubt into unshakable resilience.
- **Positive Self-Talk – Rewiring Your Mindset:** Your thoughts create your reality. This section helps you silence your inner critic, adopt empowering language, and establish habits that reinforce a positive, growth-oriented mindset.
- **Visualisation – Making Your Dreams a Reality:** The mind is a powerful tool. Here, you will engage in a self-guided vision workshop, understand the science behind manifestation, and harness the power of emotion and belief to bring your dreams to life.
- **Embracing Abundance – "Letlotlo":** Abundance is more than material wealth; it is a mindset. This final chapter explores healing, post-traumatic growth, and stepping into wholeness, teaching you how to attract opportunities and live a thriving, fulfilled life.

Whether you are an individual seeking healing and clarity, a leader aiming to foster resilience in the workplace, or someone navigating a major life transition, *The Path of Pearl* will equip you with the wisdom, guidance, and strategies to rebuild, transform, and thrive.

Writing this book has always been a dream of mine, and bringing it to life is a testament to the power of perseverance. As a driven and determined person, I want this book to serve as an inspiration to anyone with a dream, proving that no matter what challenges you face, you can rise above them.

Why *The Path of Pearl*?

A pearl is not formed overnight. It begins as an irritation, a grain of sand within an oyster, and through time, pressure, and resilience, it transforms into something rare and beautiful. Much like the pearl, our growth is shaped by life's challenges. It is in adversity that we find our strength, in uncertainty that we learn trust, and in struggle that we cultivate wisdom.

This book is not just *The Path of Pearl*; it is my path, a journey of perseverance, empowerment, healing, and transformation. My sisters named me *Pearl*, perhaps unknowingly speaking into existence the journey I would one day take, one of refinement, resilience, and emerging stronger through life's trials. My mother named me *Letlotlo*, which means *abundance*, a constant reminder that even after hardship, a life of fulfilment, joy, and wholeness is possible. These names are not just labels; they are reflections of my story, my mission, and the wisdom I now share with you.

Like the pearl, you, too, have the power to transform. You can cultivate resilience, step into your own strength, and embrace the abundance that awaits you. This book is an invitation to walk that path, to let go of what no longer serves you, to keep moving forward with faith, and to rise stronger than ever before.

To embody the essence of this journey, PEARL unfolds as:

- **P – Perseverance** in the face of adversity
- **E – Empowerment** through self-belief and confidence
- **A – Abundance** in mindset, healing, and opportunities
- **R – Resilience** to rise stronger after life's storms
- **L – Letting** go of fear, doubt, and what no longer serves you

This book is a reflection of my path, but it is also your guide to embracing growth, resilience, and abundance. Writing this book has always been a dream of mine, and now that it has come to life,

I hope it serves as a beacon of inspiration, reminding you that no matter the obstacles you face, you, too, can rise, thrive, and create a life filled with purpose and possibility.

Your transformation starts now. Let's walk this path together.

Pearl Letlotlo Olesitse

HOW TO USE THIS BOOK

Buy yourself a personal journal to use in conjunction with this book. This will give you the time and space to jot down your thoughts and ideas.

In addition, throughout the book, you will find journaling prompts.

PART 1

LETTING GO

Embracing the Power of Release

"Letting go is to love yourself enough to look at the past with a different perspective. It is to accept that you can't change the past, but you can change whether your perspective poisons or nourishes you."

Steve Maraboli (1975–)
American behavioural scientist and author

LETTING GO IS OFTEN SPOKEN of, read about, and even encouraged, but what does it truly mean? To "let go" is more than a phrase. It's a profound emotional and mental process that involves releasing the lingering attachments and resentments that weigh us down and affect our psychological well-being.

Imagine facing a detour on your life's journey: unexpected, confusing, and perhaps overwhelming. Finding your way out of these detours requires immense courage: the courage to release pain, worry, and doubt, and to embrace the act of letting go.

Letting go is an act of self-love. It is the willingness to view the past through a different lens, acknowledging that while we cannot change what has happened, we can choose whether our memories will infect us or nourish us.

Consider this famous story of two Buddhist monks travelling together[1]. Along their journey, they encountered a swift but shallow river that they needed to cross. A young woman stood on the bank, clearly afraid to cross on her own, and asked for their help. The monks had taken vows to never touch a woman, a strict observance of their Theravada tradition. One monk hesitated, bound by his vow. The other, however, compassionately picked up the woman and carried her across the river, setting her down gently on the other side.

The monks continued their journey in silence. After some time, the monk who had hesitated finally spoke up, saying, "You took vows to never touch a woman! How could you have picked her up like that?"

His companion calmly replied, "Brother, I set her down at least an hour ago. Why are you still carrying her?"

This parable offers a powerful metaphor for our own lives. How often do we carry the burdens of our past, resentments, fears, and grudges, long after the moment has passed? These lingering attachments drain our energy and hinder our ability to live a fulfilled and happy life. We may find ourselves stuck, blaming others or circumstances for our unhappiness, when in reality, the key to moving forward lies within **us**.

Saying Goodbye: The First Step to Letting Go

"If you are brave enough to say goodbye,
life will reward you with a new hello."

Paulo Coelho (1947–),
Brazilian novelist and lyricist

Letting go begins with the courage to say goodbye. This isn't solely about severing ties with people or situations; it's about releasing the negative emotions, thoughts, and habits that no longer serve you. It's about freeing yourself from the mental and emotional baggage that holds you back. It is not about forgetting or dismissing your past but about choosing to no longer let it define you or dictate your future. It's about saying goodbye to the things that weigh you down, so you can embrace the things that lift you up.

Your Turn

So, what are you ready to say goodbye to? Open your journal and take a moment to write each thought down. With each goodbye, know that you're making room for the new hello that life is ready to offer you.

Now that you've taken the time to list the things you want to say goodbye to, let me share my own journey of letting go. I'll walk you through what I had to say goodbye to and how I managed to do it. You might find that some of my experiences resonate with your own, and perhaps they'll offer you a sense of connection and encouragement on your path to letting go.

Each of us carries the weight of painful memories, those moments from our early years that still haunt us. Sometimes, all it takes is a song, a familiar place, or hearing someone else's story to trigger a flood of emotions we thought we had buried long ago. These are the wounds we hold onto, the scars that have, in some ways, become a part of our identity. The idea of letting go can be terrifying because it feels like losing a part of ourselves. But what if I told you that letting go is the key to unlocking your true potential, to finding peace and freedom?

My Story

It all began when I was five years old. Born and raised in Botswana, I was very close to my eldest sisters, who are twins, and I followed them everywhere they went. During our frequent visits to a particular family, I began to notice something that deeply confused me. Whenever we were introduced, the adults would say, "These are John's twins," without ever acknowledging me in the same way. It was as if I didn't exist. I would stand there, feeling invisible, frustrated, and isolated, until one of my sisters would kindly add, "And this is our sister." This pattern continued for some time, and I began to question my place in the world. It was clear to me, even at that young age, that John was not my father.

At the age of fourteen, I was given a school assignment titled 'Who Am I?'. It was a simple question, but it stirred something deep within me. I knew I needed answers, and so, for the first time, I gathered the courage to ask my mother about my father. In those days, especially in Botswana, asking your mother about your absent father was almost a taboo. It wasn't a conversation people had easily or openly. But I had to know.

When I finally asked, I could see the discomfort in my mother's eyes. She hesitated, not knowing what to say or how much to reveal. She told me who my father was, but said she'd give me more details when I was older, when I turned eighteen. It was clear that she didn't even know if he was still alive.

Time, as it often does, flew by. Before I knew it, I was eighteen, and the questions that had been simmering in the back of my mind for years came rushing to the surface. One day, I turned to my mother and asked her everything I needed to know. "What was my father's name? Where did he come from? Does he even know I exist?"

She answered my questions as best she could. I learned that my father had left when I was just three weeks old. The realisation that he had abandoned me so early in life was a heavy burden to carry. But I didn't stop there. At the age of twenty, I finally managed to locate my father, only to discover that I was not the only child he had abandoned. The anger and hurt I felt were overwhelming. How could someone so easily walk away from their own child?

The anger I harboured towards my father began to affect every aspect of my life, especially how I viewed men. I found it difficult to trust them, to believe in their intentions. Growing up in Botswana, where it was sadly common for fathers to abandon their children, this experience reinforced my distrust and made it even harder for me to let go of the pain. The absence of a father leaves a deep psychological impact, one that can shape your entire world-view.

But here's what I've learned: holding onto that pain only weighed me down. It kept me trapped in a cycle of anger and mistrust. Letting go, though difficult, was the only way to free myself from the past. It didn't mean forgetting what happened or pretending it didn't hurt. It meant acknowledging the pain, understanding how it shaped me, and then choosing to move forward without letting it define my future.

Letting go isn't about losing a part of yourself; it's about reclaiming your power and writing a new chapter in your life. It's about finding the strength to forgive, not for the sake of the person who hurt you, but for your own peace and well-being. It's about freeing yourself from the chains of the past so you can fully embrace the present and all the possibilities the future holds.

As you continue reading this chapter, I invite you to think about the pain you're holding onto. What memories still haunt you? What stories do you keep telling yourself that no longer serve you? And most importantly, what would your life look like if you chose to let go?

The journey to letting go is not easy, but it is worth it. It's a journey of healing, of rediscovering who you are without the weight of past hurts dragging you down. And it's a journey that leads to a place of peace, where you can finally breathe freely and live fully. So, let go. Not for anyone else, but for yourself. Let go and give yourself the gift of a future unburdened by the past.

Realising that this anger had a huge influence on my relationships, I decided to learn to let go of my father from my life, accept it as it is, and move on. However, it is often the case that you might think you have let go and then something comes up to trigger that anger.

Hence, it is important to note that holding on to negative emotions, which in my case were anger and frustration towards something I had no control over, can have a negative impact in our lives, and overtime it can affect our long-term health too.

Top Tips To Help You Let Go of Negative Emotions and Move Forward

Mindset Magic

1. **Identify the Emotion**

   Take a moment to pinpoint what you're really feeling. Is it anger, jealousy, or resentment? Sometimes, when emotions run high, it's easy to label everything as anger when, in reality, you might be feeling frustrated or disappointed. Accurately identifying your emotions is a crucial step in learning how to manage them effectively.

2. **Remember, Emotions Aren't Good or Bad**

   Emotions, even the uncomfortable ones, serve a purpose. Fear, for instance, is often viewed negatively, but it can also protect you from danger. Anger can signal that something in your life needs to change. Instead of categorising emotions as good or bad, try to understand their role in your experience.

3. **Feel the Emotion Without Judgement**

   Allow yourself to fully experience the emotion without rushing to act on it. Observe how it feels in your body; maybe your shoulders tense or your face heats up. By simply acknowledging the emotion, you can begin to accept it and give yourself permission to release it.

4. **Offer Yourself Perspective**

   Coaching yourself through difficult emotions can be incredibly helpful. Try saying, "This is tough, but feeding my anger won't change anything," or "I've felt this way before, and it passed. This will too." This kind of self-talk can shift your perspective and help you manage your emotions more effectively.

5. **Practice Releasing the Emotion**

   Letting go doesn't mean ignoring or escaping your feelings. It means acknowledging them, accepting them, and then choosing not to carry them with you. Like the story of the two Buddhist monks above, once you've carried the emotion as far as it needs to go, it's time to set it down and move on.

Action Steps

1. **Controlled Breathing Exercises**
    - Inhale through your nose for a count of three.
    - Hold your breath for a count of two.
    - Exhale through your mouth for a count of four.
    - Repeat this cycle four times.
2. **The "Cleansing Breath"**
    - Take a deep breath in through your nose, imagining the air coming in as clean, cool, and refreshing.
    - Exhale through your mouth, picturing the breath carrying out all the tension and negative feelings inside you.
    - Repeat four times.

Letting Go of Stories

We all carry stories we tell ourselves – narratives shaped by past experiences that often hinder our growth. These stories might stem from painful events, frustrations, or failures, and can hold us back from pursuing what we truly want.

For instance, you might be in a job you dislike or a relationship that's unhealthy. The story you tell yourself could be, "I can't leave because I'm too old," or "I've tried everything, but nothing works." These narratives, often ingrained from childhood, replay in our minds, shaping our present and future in limiting ways.

Consider a few common stories:

- "I am unlucky in love."

- "I'm too old/too young."
- "No one in my family has a degree, so I'm not capable."
- "I'm overweight, and I lack willpower."

These stories create self-fulfilling prophecies. For example, if you believe you're not intelligent, you might avoid challenging situations, reinforcing that belief. Or if you think you lack willpower, you might overindulge, proving your story right. The key is to recognise these narratives for what they are: stories, not facts. By challenging and rewriting these stories, you can free yourself from their hold and open up to new possibilities.

Letting go is an act of self-love. It's about releasing the past and its grip on you, choosing to view it with a perspective that nourishes rather than poisons your future. It's not about forgetting; it's about freeing yourself to grow, heal, and embrace new beginnings.

What Stories Played in My Mind? How Did I Manage To Stop the Record From Repeating Itself?

Reflecting on the story I shared about my father's absence, I realise how deeply that experience shaped my identity. For years, I fed my mind a narrative that men couldn't be trusted, and this fear became a defining part of who I was. The story I told myself wasn't just about my father's abandonment, it was a story that echoed in my relationships, in how I saw myself, and in the choices I made. It was a story that cast a long shadow over my life.

Jed Diamond, a family and marriage therapist, explores this very issue in his book, *My Distant Dad: Healing the Family Father Wound*[2]. He shares his own personal experiences of having an absent father, highlighting how the trauma of that absence can foster deep-seated fear and anxiety. Diamond discusses what he calls the "father wound," a hurt that can become a generational issue, affecting everything in our lives, and, most critically, our intimate relationships. He believes that the key to breaking this cycle of hurt and misunderstanding is recognising what belongs in the past and what belongs in the present.

For most of my life, I carried that wound with me. It was an ever-present ache, a wound that seemed to define me. I believed that men were not to be trusted, that they would leave just as my father did. This belief wasn't simply a passing thought, but was a story that shaped my interactions, my fears, and my sense of self. It became a part of my identity, something I clung to even as it held me back.

In *The Power of Letting Go*[3], John Purkiss emphasises the importance of living in the moment and then releasing it, rather than clinging to it. He suggests that our tendency to label experiences and assemble them into stories often leads to more pain. I can deeply relate to his perspective.

But here's the truth: everyone's story is different, yet the pain of an absent parent, whether through physical absence or emotional distance, leaves a profound lack. It creates a void that we often try to fill with stories that justify our pain, stories that help us make sense of our hurt. These stories can feel safe, like a well-worn blanket we wrap ourselves in for comfort. But over time, that blanket becomes suffocating. The stories we tell ourselves can become chains that keep us tied to the past, preventing us from fully living in the present.

It wasn't until my late thirties that I made the decision to let go of the story I had been telling myself for so long. I realised that in order to heal, I needed to release the narrative that men couldn't be trusted. I had to let go of the identity I had formed around that belief. This wasn't an easy process; it required deep introspection and a willingness to confront the pain I had carried for so many years. But it was also incredibly freeing.

Letting go doesn't mean erasing the past. It means acknowledging it, understanding how it has shaped you, and then choosing to release its hold on your present and future. It's about recognising that while your past experiences are a part of your story, they don't have to define you. You have the power to rewrite your narrative, to choose a new story, one that reflects your growth, your resilience, and your desire to live a life unburdened by old wounds.

As you read this, I invite you to consider the stories you've been telling yourself. Are they still serving you? Are they helping you to grow, or are they keeping you stuck in the past? Letting go of these stories is not about denying your experiences; it's about choosing to live in the present, to embrace the person you are today, and to create a future that is not dictated by the wounds of yesterday.

Healing from the wounds of parental absence or divorce is a deeply personal journey, but it's also one that holds the potential for immense growth and transformation. Here are some steps that can guide you through the process of letting go and embracing a more fulfilling life.

Step 1: Believe in Your Power to Heal

The first and most crucial step in your healing journey is to believe that you have the power to heal. No matter what trauma or pain you've experienced, you possess an unshakable wholeness within you. This inner strength enables you to grow, transform, forgive, and, ultimately, heal. It's easy to feel powerless in the face of deep wounds but remember that you create your own reality. By acknowledging this power, you take responsibility for your healing and open the door to the life you deserve.

Step 2: Seek Help

Healing doesn't mean you have to do it alone. One of the bravest things you can do is to allow yourself to be vulnerable and share your story. Seeking assistance from therapists or healing professionals is not a sign of weakness, it's an act of empowerment.

By reaching out for help, you're taking responsibility for your life and demonstrating a commitment to your own well-being. Remember, healing is a journey that is often made easier with guidance and support from those who are trained to help you navigate the complexities of your emotions and experiences.

Step 3: Cultivate Self-Awareness

Understanding yourself is a key component of healing. Self-awareness, as defined in the philosophy of self, is the experience of one's own personality and individuality. It's the ability to look inward and understand who you are, why you behave the way you do, and how your experiences have shaped you. Often, we avoid introspection because it can be uncomfortable or even painful to confront our deepest fears and insecurities. However, by facing these uncomfortable truths, we gain insight into the behavioural tendencies and emotional impacts stemming from having an absent parent. With this understanding, you can choose how to respond to your pain in a way that prioritises self-love, control, and wisdom.

Step 4: Forgive, Let Go, and Trust

Blame is a heavy burden to carry, whether it is directed at ourselves or others. When we hold onto blame, we remain stuck, unable to fully embrace the blessings that life has to offer. I once blamed my mother for having me with a man who wasn't present in my life. I blamed my father's absence for making me feel unworthy of love and for my struggles in maintaining lasting relationships. But the truth is, no amount of blame can change the past. What happened, happened. The only thing we can control is how we choose to move forward.

Forgiveness is the key to releasing this burden. Start by forgiving yourself. Stop the cycle of blame and instead, focus on being thankful for the lessons you've learned along the way. Forgiving your parents, whether for their absence, their choices, or their mistakes, is essential in letting go. When you forgive, you open yourself up to trust the process of life, to embrace challenges as opportunities for growth, and to recognise your own capacity for love.

Forgiveness isn't easy, but it's essential for healing. It allows you to let go of the past and focus on the bigger picture of life, a life filled with possibilities, love, and the freedom to be your true self.

As you work through these steps in your journal, remember that healing is a journey, not a destination. It's about progress, not perfection. By believing in your power to heal, seeking help when you need it, cultivating self-awareness, and embracing forgiveness, you'll find that the weight of the past begins to lift, leaving you free to create a brighter, more fulfilling future.

Call to Action

Here is a powerful exercise to help you let go of negative stories. In your journal, write down a story that you keep telling yourself or others, then answer the following questions:

- What are the limiting beliefs underlying the story?
- Do you get pleasure/comfort from repeating the story to yourself?
- How is this story holding you back from what you want?
- What will be the benefit to you from letting go of this story now?

Letting Go of Fear of Change

"It is not the strongest of the species that survives, nor the most intelligent, but the one most adaptable to change."

Charles Darwin (1809–1882)
British naturalist and biologist

Have you ever felt like fear is holding you back from reaching your goals? That the fear of the unknown keeps you stuck, unable to make the changes you know you need? Many people feel this way, whether they're stuck in a job they dislike, trapped in an unfulfilling relationship, or facing other situations that no longer serve them. The common thread is fear, the kind that paralyses us and makes us cling to what's familiar, even if it's not what we truly want.

But what is fear?

The *Cambridge Dictionary* defines it as *"an unpleasant emotion or thought that you have when you are frightened or worried by something dangerous, painful, or bad that is happening or might happen."* [4]

Fear of change, or metathesiophobia, is more than a reluctance to try new things; it's a deep-seated phobia that keeps us from moving forward. This fear is often linked with tropophobia, the fear of moving. As humans, it's natural to feel apprehensive about anything that pushes us out of our comfort zone. But if we want to live a life that reflects our best possibilities, we must embrace change as a natural part of our evolution.

Ever since I was a little girl, I've been fascinated by the capabilities of human beings. This fascination fuelled my desire to try new things and make changes in my life whenever my circumstances no longer aligned with my goals. I dreamed of living abroad and changing my profession, but I knew that to achieve these dreams, I had to be willing to take bold steps.

In 2002, I secured a place at Botswana's top university to study for a Bachelor of Science, with hopes of doing well enough to earn a scholarship to study medicine abroad. However, when my first-year results came out, they were good, but not good enough. I felt frustrated and disappointed, as if I had let myself and my family down. I even considered giving up on my studies entirely.

But my mother, ever supportive, reminded me that this setback wasn't the end of the world. She encouraged me to return to college and pursue something else, and that's what I did. I decided to study nursing, and upon graduation, I began working at one of Botswana's largest referral hospitals. I became a confident paediatric nurse, thriving in a supportive team despite the common challenges of bullying and the high-pressure environment.

One day, while looking through a newspaper, I came across an article about a new state-of-the-art hospital looking for nurses. The position required more than two years of experience, and I was just shy of that mark, but I decided to apply anyway. Some of my colleagues laughed at my ambition, pointing out my lack of experience, but I didn't let their doubts sway me. I was confident that I had the skills needed, and I pressed forward with my application.

And I was right. I got the job, which allowed me to gain valuable experience while I continued to explore ways to fulfil my dream of living and working abroad. After five years of working in local hospitals, I knew it was time to make a change once more. I started researching how to find a job abroad as a nurse, gathering all the information I needed to make my move.

For nearly six years, I worked towards this goal. Then, in June 2012, I had a chance encounter that changed everything. While at a shopping centre, I bumped into a former lecturer whose niece happened to mention that she was going to study in Dublin, Ireland. Intrigued, I approached her and asked how she managed it. She explained the process and gave me the contact details of the agency that helped her. Without hesitation, I contacted them.

By August 2012, I was on a flight to Dublin, ready to further my studies and explore new professional opportunities. If I had let fear control me, I would still be stuck in the same place, living a life that no longer served me.

In writing this book, I've spoken to many nurses who are unhappy in their workplaces but are too afraid of change to take the next step. I understand that fear. But I also know that on the other side of that fear is the life you've always dreamed of. Change can be intimidating, but it's also necessary for growth. It's the key to unlocking new opportunities and living a life that reflects your true potential.

So, ask yourself: What's holding you back? What changes are you afraid to make? And how might your life be different if you let go of that fear and embraced the possibilities that change can bring?

Letting Go of Control

It is now time to embrace the change, trust the process, and accept that you can't always dictate what happens, but you can control how you respond. Letting go of control is one of the most challenging yet liberating acts you can undertake. As human beings, we crave certainty. We want to know the outcomes, predict the future, and steer the course of our lives in the direction we think is best. However, life doesn't always adhere to our carefully crafted plans, and the need for control can create tension, frustration, and anxiety.

For me, learning to let go of control was a process tied to one of the biggest transitions in my life. After already dealing with the story of an absent father and navigating through a web of mistrust and scepticism towards men, I had managed to let go of the narrative that had kept me guarded, which was hard enough. But when it was time to make the leap and leave my home country to pursue a career outside of nursing, what I had been trained in, and realise my dreams, letting go of control became even more challenging. I found myself in a situation where I was not only navigating unfamiliar territory professionally, but also facing personal uncertainty.

Imagine having grown up with a certain degree of control over your environment, a stable job, a close-knit family, and a familiar home that brings you comfort. You know your routine, your surroundings, and what to expect from life, day after day. This sense of security provides a feeling of safety, even if deep down, something inside you whispers that there might be more – more opportunities, more growth, more potential – for the life you truly desire.

Now imagine standing on the edge of this safe, familiar life, looking out into the unknown. The idea of leaving behind your secure job, the family and friends who surround you, and the comforts of the home you've always known, can feel terrifying. Taking that leap of faith means stepping into uncertainty, where you have no control over what happens next. It's a place where outcomes are unknown, challenges are inevitable, and security is not guaranteed. The fear of losing control is natural, and yet, this moment holds the key to true growth.

Letting go of control doesn't mean abandoning responsibility or becoming passive about your future. Instead, it means trusting the process, believing in your ability to navigate whatever life brings your way, and having faith that sometimes, the best outcomes come from the paths you hadn't planned. When you release the need to micromanage every aspect of your life, you make room for the unexpected blessings that come when you least expect them.

I remember facing this decision, to leave behind the familiar and pursue a new life in a foreign country. I had spent years in a structured environment, where I knew exactly what was required of me each day. I had a clear sense of purpose, but over time, a new dream began to emerge, a calling to explore a different life.

Leaving my nursing career, my family, especially my mother, and stepping into the unknown, felt as if I was standing on a cliff's edge, not knowing if there would be solid ground beneath my feet once I jumped.

The moment I made the decision to leave, I quickly realised how much control I was giving up. I couldn't predict what would happen next, whether I would succeed in my new path, whether I'd find my footing in a new country, or whether the sacrifices I made would pay off. The fear of failure crept in, and I found myself questioning whether I should turn back to the safety of what I knew.

But here's what I learned: letting go of control is where transformation happens. The greatest growth happens not when you're holding on tight, but when you trust yourself enough to let go.

Take a moment to reflect on your own life. Is there something you're holding onto tightly – an idea, a job, or a way of living – because it gives you a sense of control? What might happen if you loosened your grip and embraced the possibility that things might unfold in ways you can't yet foresee? Letting go of control is not about giving up; it's about opening yourself to the full spectrum of what life has to offer. Life is full of unpredictable moments, and trying to control everything is not only impossible but exhausting. Letting go of control opens us to greater possibilities, helps us find peace amid chaos, and ultimately gives us the freedom to live life more fully.

As you move forward, remember this: you don't have to control every step of the journey to reach your destination. Trust yourself to handle whatever comes, and have faith that sometimes, the most meaningful experiences happen when you let go and allow life to guide you.

Ho'oponopono Prayer

In her article, 'The Ho'oponopono Power of Forgiveness and Letting Go,' Kathy Gottberg[5] introduces Ho'oponopono, an ancient Hawaiian practice used to cleanse negative memories, unconscious fears, and unhelpful mental patterns. Taught by the Hawaiian Kahuna, or wise elders, this prayer aims to restore inner peace and balance. Gottberg shares a Hawaiian legend that beautifully illustrates this: every child is born with a "bowl of light," representing qualities like love, creativity, and playfulness. But as we grow, we begin to fill this bowl with anger, fear, worry, and regret, each negative emotion akin to a stone. Over time, the light becomes overshadowed by these burdens, turning us into something heavier, more rigid, like a stone. Yet, through the practice of Ho'oponopono, we have the power to release these accumulated weights, gradually allowing our light to shine through once more.

You can find the prayer on YouTube.[6]

PEARLS OF WISDOM

Techniques for Letting Go of the Fear of Change

If you're ready to let go of the fear of change, here are some powerful techniques to help you along your journey.

Accept the Situation, But Don't Resign to It

Acceptance is the first step towards change, but it doesn't mean surrendering to your current circumstances. When I realised I wasn't where I wanted to be, I accepted that reality, but I didn't allow it to define my future. Acceptance requires courage, determination, and honesty. It's about recognising where you are without becoming a passive victim of circumstances. You have the power to change your life, but it starts with acknowledging where you stand.

Change Your Mindset: See Failure as a Positive

One of the greatest obstacles to embracing change is the fear of failure. When I didn't secure a scholarship to study medicine abroad, it felt like a major setback. But over time, I learned that everything happens for a reason. During my nursing studies, I began to view failure as a stepping stone rather than a stumbling block. Psychologist Carol Dweck[7], in her work on the growth mindset, teaches us that those who see challenges and failures as opportunities for growth are more likely to succeed. By shifting my mindset to see failure as a natural part of the journey, I freed myself from the emotional baggage that was holding me back. I started to enjoy the process of learning and growing, rather than fixating on the destination.

Step Outside Your Comfort Zone

Entering our zone of freedom and letting go of the fear of failure doesn't require radical changes. You can start by gradually training your mind to think differently. Repeat affirmations like, "This is not where I want to be, and sooner or later, I'm out of here." Many people, especially in professions such as nursing, feel trapped in a mental space where routine and job security create an illusion of safety. Yet they remain unhappy because they've confined themselves to this comfort zone. To break free, attend conferences that align with your passions, network with people outside your immediate circle, and expose yourself to new ideas. This will help you see that change is possible and that you're not bound by your current situation.

Practise Patience

Change doesn't happen overnight, just as success takes time. On your journey towards change, you'll encounter turbulence and challenges that may test your resolve. This is where patience comes into play. When I was frustrated about not getting the scholarship to study medicine, I wanted to give up on university entirely. But after talking to my mother, I learned the value of patience. I stayed on course with my nursing studies and continued working until the right opportunity presented itself. Patience isn't only about waiting; it's about maintaining a positive attitude and staying focused on your goals, even when progress seems slow.

Do Your Research: Look for Evidence

If you're contemplating a change but feel paralysed by the fear of the unknown, do your research. Talk to people who have made similar changes, read books on the subject, and gather as much information as you can. When I decided to move abroad, I spent time researching how to find a nursing job overseas. This preparation made the process feel less daunting and more manageable. The more you know, the more confident you'll feel about taking the next step.

Take Action

Once you've accepted your situation, changed your mindset, stepped outside your comfort zone, practised patience, and done your research, it's time to take action. Daily meditation, such as practicing Ho'oponopono, can help you release negative thoughts and emotions. Create affirmations that resonate with your goals and repeat them until they become part of your belief system. Visualise yourself as the person you want to be after letting go of what's holding you back. Focus on what brings you joy, and use that positive energy to fuel your transformation.

A significant part of our long-term happiness and success hinges on our ability to let go of what we think life is supposed to be right now and to appreciate it for what it is. By doing so, we can focus on the things within our control and release the things we can't control. Letting go frees our minds from needless worries and opens up space for growth and healing. When we allow ourselves to let go, we give ourselves the gift of personal evolution and the chance to embrace the life we truly desire.

PART 2

KEEP ON KEEPING ON

THIS IS A PHRASE WE'VE ALL heard, but what does it truly mean? The *Cambridge Dictionary* defines to 'keep on keeping on' as *"continuing with what you are doing or trying to achieve, especially when this is difficult or unpleasant"*.[8] It's a call to persistence, a reminder that when life gets tough, the tough do not give up, but keep moving forward.

When soldiers head into battle, they're equipped with everything they need to endure the hardships ahead. They're prepared to face obstacles and challenges, no matter how daunting, because they have a mission, a reason that drives them forward. Similarly, in our own lives, we embark on journeys with a destination in mind, armed with our goals, dreams, and aspirations. Life, as they say, is a journey, and on this path, we encounter potholes, hills, rivers, mountains, and valleys that test our resolve.

Imagine setting out on a road trip. You've checked your car, packed your essentials, and set your GPS to your chosen destination. As you drive, the road starts to narrow, winding precariously with potholes at every turn. Then, a storm hits, heavy rain obscures your vision, making it hard to see what's ahead. What do you do? Do you turn back? Do you stop, hoping the road will magically clear up? Of course not! You keep driving, pressing on through the storm because you know *why* you're on this journey in the first place. You might pause, waiting for the worst of the storm to pass, but you never lose sight of your destination.

In life, storms are inevitable. Challenges will arise that shake your confidence and make you question your path. But it's in these moments that you must remember your why. Whether your goal is to achieve a better quality of life, to reach your career aspirations, or to fulfil a personal dream, the journey will test you. The key is to keep on keeping on, no matter how difficult the road becomes. Here's a simple truth: life's challenges are like the potholes and storm on that treacherous road. They're part of the journey, not the end of it. The ability to persist, to soldier on through the turbulence, is what will ultimately get you to your destination.

Take a moment to reflect on your own journey. What are the challenges that have made you want to turn back? What storms have clouded your vision and made you doubt your ability to reach your goals? Perhaps it's been a career setback, a personal loss, or a health challenge. Whatever it is, know that you have the strength to keep moving forward.

This chapter invites you to embrace the mindset of persistence. To keep on keeping on, even when the road is tough. Remember, you are equipped for this journey. Your *why* is your compass, guiding you through the storms and leading you to your destination.

In the following table, I've outlined some common life challenges and how they require us to keep on keeping on. Use it as a reference, a reminder that no matter what comes your way, you have the strength to keep moving forward. Why not copy the table into your journal?

Health and wellness issues	Immigration status	Divorce / separations	Disabilities
Injustice	Fraud	Oppression	Poverty
Racism	Social exclusion	Accidents	Rejection
Mistakes	Shame	Grief and loss	Unemployment / job insecurity

Have you experienced any of the above? Or perhaps you are experiencing one of them now? How did you feel when faced with the obstacles that seemed insurmountable? Did you ever consider giving up on your goals? What did you do to propel yourself forward in the face of adversity? These are the questions I want you to reflect on and make notes about as we dive deeper into the concept of keeping on keeping on.

In the previous chapter, I shared the dream that ignited a fire within me, the dream to relocate abroad, to further my studies, and to eventually change my career path. This journey was not smooth. The road was filled with mountains to climb, valleys to navigate, and storms that threatened to derail me. But through it all, I held onto my why, the purpose that kept me going, even when the challenges seemed overwhelming.

One of the most powerful reminders of this perseverance comes from the Bob Dylan song *Tangled Up In Blue*[9], recorded in January1975.

Dylan sings:

The only thing I knew how to do
was to keep on keepin' on, like a bird that flew

These words resonate deeply with me and I'm sure with many others who have faced their own trials and tribulations.

Dylan's lyrics capture the essence of resilience, the ability to keep moving forward, even when the path is unclear, and the skies are stormy. Like that bird, you may find yourself tangled up in the blue, lost in the complexities of life's challenges. But the key is to keep flying, to keep on keeping on, no matter how tangled the situation may seem.

Reflect on your own journey. Think about the moments when you felt tangled up in the blue. What kept you going? Was it the support of loved ones, a deep-seated belief in your goals, or simply the refusal to give up? These moments, these decisions to keep moving forward, are what define us. They shape our character and bring us closer to the realisation of our dreams.

In my journey to fulfil my dream of studying and working abroad, I encountered numerous obstacles that tested my resolve. But each time, I chose to keep going. I chose to keep on keeping on, driven by the belief that my why was worth the struggle. And in doing so, I learned that persistence isn't just about enduring the challenges, it's about growing through them.

My Story

As mentioned, in 2012, I took a leap of faith and left my home, family, and career in Botswana to pursue my dreams in Ireland. What was meant to be an exciting new chapter quickly turned into a nightmare when I became a victim of a fraudulent agency. The 'agency' promised a smooth transition to college life abroad, only for me to arrive in Dublin and find myself stranded, swindled out of money by these con artists, with nothing but a place in a run-down hostel and no tuition paid.

My family was thrilled with my posting, especially my mother, though her parting words to the agency's representatives stayed with me: "I hope you are not throwing away my child." They reassured her, claiming that their own brother was also heading to Ireland. But looking back, those words carried a mother's intuition that I wished I'd heeded.

Rewinding a bit, I first learned about this opportunity through Loppy, the niece of my former lecturer, who introduced me to the agency. During their presentation, Mark, an admissions officer from the Irish college, painted a convincing picture. He spoke about the school, displayed photos of accommodations, and even mentioned flexible arrangements for housing. My family and I felt reassured by his promises, and I moved forward with payments for everything; tuition, travel, accommodation, and other expenses. Finally, after six long years of trying to relocate abroad, I was heading to Ireland, hopeful for a new beginning.

However, upon my arrival in Dublin, reality struck hard. The taxi arranged by the agency dropped me off at a shabby hostel, far from the hotel I had been promised. I quickly reached out to the agency, but they evaded my concerns, claiming everything would be resolved after the holiday weekend. Growing suspicious, I contacted Loppy, who revealed she was experiencing similar issues, despite being at a different college. Realising we had both been deceived, I launched my own investigation.

At the college, I requested a reprint of my payment records, only to find out that no payments had been made on my behalf. Even the supposed proof of accommodation used at immigration turned out to be false. Confronting Mark under the guise of needing a reimbursement for accommodation, I managed to recover a small amount, though he remained unaware that I knew the full extent of the deception. Meanwhile, Loppy faced a similar revelation at her institution, where she learned that her tuition and health insurance were also unpaid.

Determined to seek justice and prevent others from falling into the same trap, Loppy and I returned to Botswana with our evidence, filing reports with the police. Despite our best efforts, we encountered systemic indifference and corruption, which allowed the women behind the scam to evade consequences.

The trip back home served as a painful reminder of the systems that often fail those who need them most. But even then, the setback didn't break my resolve. I returned to Ireland after two weeks of back and forth with the law authorities in Botswana, determined to salvage what I could from the situation.

Returning to Ireland, I faced yet another challenge when the authorities abruptly shut down the fraudulent colleges, including the one where Loppy was enrolled. I remember when I then decided to call my mother, hoping for comfort, her simple but profound advice was, "Go and look for a reputable college and finish what you went there for." Her words echoed her belief that obstacles are inevitable, but perseverance is key. Ausi, as we called my mother, always looked beyond challenges, focusing on the end goal.

Once again, I found myself at a crossroads: no college, no clear path forward, my savings drained, and my future shrouded in uncertainty. Yet, amidst the confusion, the student visa constraints were lifted, so I worked as a full-time carer, as I was not yet a registered nurse in Ireland, to regain some financial stability. While many international students made the difficult decision to return home, I resolved to stay and rebuild my life in Ireland, determined not to let this setback define me.

But as I grappled with the college closure, another blow came: the passing of my uncle. The grief and the weight of all that had happened became overwhelming, and I realised that I needed a break from the relentless challenges. I made the decision to return home to Botswana for a month to rest, reflect, and find the strength to restart my journey once more. It was a time to regain my footing, reconnect with my roots, and gather the resilience I would need to face the road ahead.

Reflecting on those early days, I realise that my journey was not about being swindled, it was about learning to fight for my dreams even when the path was crooked and unclear. The fraudulent agency, the closed college, and the indifferent authorities each challenge sharpened my resolve.

Rest

As we push forward through life's challenges, there will inevitably be days when the best course of action is to take a step back, breathe, and rest. Sometimes, the mental toughness required to stay committed to our goals can be overwhelming, especially when nothing seems to be going as planned.

Your Turn

Think back to a time when you were overwhelmed by a situation and felt like giving up. In the space below, jot down the thoughts that came to mind, then add them to your journal.

While you're reflecting, consider these common thoughts that might help trigger your memory:

- "I can't do this anymore."
- "Why do I have to go through this?"
- "I have nothing to live for."
- "This job is not for me."
- "I wish I could disappear."
- "What's the point of life?"

We've all experienced moments when these thoughts take over, repeating endlessly in our minds. For me, it was often the nagging refrain of "I can't do this anymore" and "Why do I have to go through this?" I'm sure you can relate. But the real question is, how do you pull yourself out of this mental spiral and refocus on positive thoughts?

Researchers have explored the concept of rest and how it manifests in daily life. An exploratory study on rest found that its definition varies from person to person and can involve any number of activities. Rest, in essence, can be seen as:

- Freedom from mental stress and relaxation
- Freedom to do what you enjoy
- Pleasure in performance or accomplishment
- Restoration of energy and focus

Rest can take on many forms, from simply calming your mind and body, to engaging in activities that bring you joy and a sense of balance. It's more than physical relaxation; it's about "letting go, in confidence."

Letting Go, in Confidence

So, what does it mean to let go, in confidence? As humans, we live with constant responsibilities that can sometimes feel overwhelming. Rest, in this context, means temporarily allowing yourself to set aside these responsibilities and experience harmony within your feelings, actions, and motivations. You leave all the demands you carry around and things you keep up with, and rest up for a while in order to cope later.

During life's most challenging moments, we often find ourselves searching for a sense of peace and renewal. When faced with overwhelming circumstances, whether it be the emotional toll of grief, the physical demands of an illness like cancer, or simply the fatigue of life's journey, there comes a time when the best path forward is to go back to where it all began.

For me, that meant returning home to Botswana, as mentioned, retracing my steps to the places and the people that could restore my strength and remind me of my purpose.

Home is more than just a physical place; it is a sanctuary where our souls can find rest, comfort, and rejuvenation. It's where we are surrounded by the familiar, the smells, the sounds, the landscapes that have shaped our identity. For many, home is where we feel most connected to ourselves, our past, and our deepest values. It is where we are reminded of who we are and why we fight so hard to overcome life's challenges.

Returning to Botswana was a deliberate choice to reconnect with the essence of who I am. The journey back was not only about seeking rest, but about reawakening the parts of myself that had been worn down by the relentless pace of life. In Botswana, I knew I would find the grounding I needed to rebuild my strength, both physically and emotionally.

My mother has always been a beacon of strength and wisdom in my life. Her presence was a constant reminder of my why, the core reason behind everything I do. In her, I found not only the comfort of a parent's love but also the clarity and motivation to keep moving forward, even when the path seemed uncertain.

Going back home meant more than just being in a familiar place; it meant being with someone who knew me intimately, who understood my struggles without needing explanations, and who could provide the emotional nourishment I desperately needed. The energy that my mother brought into my life was a powerful antidote to the exhaustion and doubt that had taken hold of me. Hence why surrounding yourself with people who rejuvenate your energy is crucial, especially during times of need. These are the people who see your potential, who encourage you to keep pushing forward, and who remind you of the dreams and aspirations that might have been overshadowed by the challenges you face. They are the ones who help you rediscover your passion, reignite your spirit, and reconnect with the reasons you started your journey in the first place.

There is something profoundly powerful about retracing your steps, about going back to the places that have shaped you, and revisiting the memories that have defined your path. In doing so, you reconnect with your roots, and in those roots, you often find the answers to the questions that have been weighing on your mind.

In Botswana, I found clarity. I was reminded of the dreams I had nurtured as a child, the values which I will discuss in detail in the next chapter, and the resilience that had carried me through previous challenges. I was able to see my life not as a series of obstacles but as a continuous journey with a clear and meaningful direction. More importantly, I was reminded of my why, the driving force behind everything I do. In that reminder, I found the motivation to continue my journey, stronger and more focused than ever before.

For anyone facing their own challenges, I encourage you to consider the power of going back to your roots to find rest. Whether it's a physical return to a place that holds meaning for you, or a reconnection with loved ones who remind you of your purpose, these moments of return can be the key to unlocking the healing and strength you need to keep moving forward.

The Art of Rejuvenation

True rest is not just about sleeping or relaxing; it's about finding ways to rejuvenate your mind, body, and spirit, especially during challenging times.

Top Tips To Help You Recharge, Reset, and Reclaim Your Energy

The Power of Meditation

Rest is about opening your mind to a state of calm. One powerful way to rejuvenate yourself is through meditation. Whether you choose to meditate alone or with others, incorporating this practice into your morning or evening routine can work wonders. There are various types of meditation to explore: mantra meditation, which involves repeating a word or phrase to aid concentration; movement meditation, which integrates gentle physical activity; and spiritual meditation, which connects you with a higher purpose. The key is to find what resonates with you and to spread calm throughout your mind, while becoming aware of how your body feels.

When I returned home to Botswana to rest and rejuvenate, I realised I needed something more than physical rest. I had heard about the benefits of meditation, and how it could calm the mind, reduce stress, and bring inner peace. Yet, at that time, meditation was a new and elusive concept for me. Despite my efforts, I struggled to quieten my mind.

The idea of meditation was appealing. I pictured myself sitting peacefully, my thoughts neatly tucked away, feeling a profound sense of calm. However, the reality was far more challenging. Each time I tried to meditate, my mind raced with thoughts, memories of the past, worries about the future, and an endless stream of mental chatter that refused to quiet down.

I would sit down with the intention to meditate, focusing on my breath or trying to clear my mind, but instead, I became acutely aware of just how noisy my thoughts were. Rather than feeling serene, I felt frustrated. The more I tried to push the thoughts away, the louder they seemed to become. It was as if my mind was resisting the very stillness I was seeking.

Through this experience, I learned that meditation, like any other skill, requires patience, practice, and a willingness to let go of expectations. I wasn't yet equipped to fully embrace the practice, but even in those moments of struggle, I learned something valuable: meditation is not about forcing the mind to be quiet, but about observing the mind without getting caught up in its activity.

Struggling with meditation is a common experience, especially for beginners. Our minds are naturally busy, constantly processing information, solving problems, and reacting to the world around us. The act of sitting quietly and doing nothing can feel unnatural or even uncomfortable, particularly when you're used to being active and productive.

In those early attempts, I was confronted with the sheer volume of my thoughts. Meditation brought awareness to the mind's activity, and the struggle to quiet the mind reflected how much I was carrying around with me. I began to understand that meditation wasn't about silencing my thoughts but changing my relationship with them. This revelation took time to fully embrace, but it sparked a curiosity to learn more.

In the chapters to come, I will delve deeper into the practice of meditation, exploring different techniques, understanding the science behind it, and sharing the insights I've gained along the way. I'll discuss how I gradually learnt to quiet my mind, not by achieving a perfect state of peace, but by finding moments of stillness amidst life's noise.

If you're struggling with meditation, my story may resonate with you. The journey to mastering meditation is not always easy, but it is one worth taking. Whether you're just beginning or have tried and felt frustrated, know that the challenges you face are part of the process. With patience and persistence, the rewards of meditation can be profound.

Finding Joy in Hobbies

When life becomes overwhelming, the most effective form of rest can often be found in the simple joy of hobbies. These activities don't have to be strenuous or time-consuming – they simply need to bring you peace and fulfilment. Whether it's painting, knitting, fishing, or playing a musical instrument, hobbies offer a way to reconnect with yourself and find solace in the present moment.

Returning home provided me with more than the comfort of familiar surroundings; it gave me the opportunity to engage in activities that brought me a sense of inner calm. Playing chess on my laptop, reading books, and cooking for my mother became more than just pastimes; they were sources of rest and restoration.

Hobbies provide a unique form of rest by allowing you to shift your focus away from stress and towards something you enjoy. These activities engage your mind differently, giving you a break from the demands and worries that often dominate your thoughts. Each time I played chess or read a book, I was able to engage in something different from my daily concerns.

Chess has always been a game that I find both challenging and relaxing. Playing on my laptop during my time at home allowed me to keep my mind sharp while also providing a much-needed distraction from stress. The game requires focus and strategy, which helped me stay present and engaged, offering a mental break from life's anxieties.

Books, too, have always been a source of comfort and knowledge for me. During my rest, I delved into reading, allowing myself to be transported into different worlds, ideas, and perspectives. This offered me both relaxation and inspiration, enriching my mind and soul. Here are a few books I'd highly recommend when you want to rejuvenate your mind, body, and spirit: *The Monk Who Sold His Ferrari* by Robin Sharma[10], *You Can Heal Your Life* by Louise Hay[11], *The Untethered Soul* by Michael A. Singer[12], *Daring Greatly* by Brené Brown[13], *The Art of Happiness* by the Dalai Lama and Howard Cutler[14], and *Wherever You Go, There You Are* by Jon Kabat-Zinn[15].

Cooking meals for myself and my mother also became a source of joy. This simple act not only brought me satisfaction but also allowed me to draw wisdom from her as we shared conversations and memories in the kitchen.

As you consider your need for rest, think about the hobbies and activities that bring you peace. Incorporate them into your daily or weekly routine as a form of active rest, a time dedicated to recharging your mind, body, and spirit. Whether you're facing a difficult time or simply need a break from the demands of everyday life, hobbies can be a powerful way to find rest.

The Healing Power of Journalling

Journalling is a powerful tool for rest, reflection, and self-discovery. It's more than simply writing words on a page; it's a way to connect deeply with your inner self, process the day's events, and find clarity amidst the chaos of life. By recording your thoughts, experiences, and observations, you create a space where your mind can unwind, and your emotions can find release.

Whether you prefer the tactile experience of writing in a physical notebook to give your eyes a break from screens, or the convenience of typing into a digital notepad, journalling offers a form of mental rest. It allows you to slow down, focus on the present moment, and explore your thoughts and feelings in a safe, private space.

Taking time each day to journal can be a deeply restorative practice. It's a moment of stillness in an otherwise busy day, a time to reflect on what you're grateful for, the things that brought you joy, your worries, or any ideas that came to mind. By dedicating a specific time each day to journalling, perhaps in the fresh air or in a peaceful corner of your home, you create a ritual that grounds you. This practice helps you clear your mind, gain insight into your emotions, and find balance in your life.

Journalling also offers a way to track your personal growth over time. By looking back at previous entries, you can see how far you've come, how your thoughts and feelings have evolved, and what patterns have emerged in your thinking. This self-awareness is crucial for personal development and emotional well-being.

• •

An Example of a Journal Entry

To give you a better understanding of what journalling might look like, here's an example of a journal entry:

Date: 10th August 2013.

Location: My favourite spot by the window, with a view of the garden.

Mood: Reflective, slightly anxious, but hopeful.

Gratitude:

- I'm grateful for the quiet morning I had today, sipping tea while the sun slowly rose. There's something so peaceful about those first moments of the day.
- I'm thankful for the conversation I had with Sarah. She always knows how to make me laugh, and it reminded me of the importance of having good friends.
- I appreciate the time I took to read today. *The Untethered Soul* is challenging my perspectives in ways I didn't expect.

Thoughts: Today felt like a whirlwind of emotions. I woke up with a sense of dread that I couldn't quite place, but as the day went on, I realised it was the result of yesterday's stressful meeting at work. I keep replaying the conversation in my head, wondering if I said the right things. It's exhausting. But writing this down makes me realise how much power I'm giving to a moment that's already passed. I can't change it, so why let it control me?

Reflections: I've been thinking a lot about the concept of letting go. It's something I struggle with: letting go of control, letting go of past mistakes, even letting go of the need to always be "on." I noticed this during my meditation practice today. My mind kept wandering back to work, back to the things I can't control. But there was a moment, just a brief one, where I felt a sense of peace, like I was floating above it all. That's the feeling I want to cultivate more.

Worries:

- I'm worried about the upcoming project deadline. I keep thinking I'm not prepared enough, but maybe that's just the anxiety talking.
- I'm also concerned about my friend. She's been distant lately, and I can't help but wonder if she's going through something. I should reach out to her tomorrow.

Ideas:

- I had a thought about starting a small garden. It could be a way to spend more time outdoors and disconnect from the digital world. I'll look into what plants are best for beginners.
- I also want to explore creative writing again. Maybe try my hand at poetry? It could be a way to express the emotions I'm not always able to articulate in conversation.

This journal entry serves as a snapshot of a moment in time, capturing a mix of gratitude, reflections, worries, and ideas. It's a way to process thoughts and emotions that might otherwise feel overwhelming if left unchecked. Through the act of journalling, you give yourself the opportunity to observe your mind, recognise patterns, and find solutions to the challenges you face.

Call to Action

Take a moment today to pause, reflect, and, in your journal or the following space provided, put pen to paper, whether it's in the quiet of the morning, or after a busy day. Start small – write a few lines about your mood, something you're grateful for, or a worry that's been on your mind. There's no right or wrong way to journal, and it doesn't have to be perfect.

Challenge yourself to embrace this practice, even for a few minutes a day. Notice how your perspective and energy shifts as you begin to clear mental clutter, find clarity, and reconnect with yourself.

Start Your Journal!

By regularly engaging in this practice, you not only rest your mind but also nurture your emotional and mental well-being. Whether you write every day or only when you feel the need, journalling is a powerful way to connect with yourself, find clarity, and cultivate a deeper sense of peace in your life.

Daily Rituals for Rest

Finally, consider incorporating daily rituals that bring you comfort and ease. Daily rituals are habits or routines that you engage in regularly, often at the same time each day. What makes them so effective for rest is their consistency and the sense of comfort they bring. When you engage in a familiar activity that you enjoy, it becomes a moment of calm, a pause in the day where you can breathe, reset, and find a sense of balance.

These rituals don't have to be elaborate. In fact, the simpler they are, the more easily they can be integrated into your daily life. The key is to choose something that resonates with you personally, an activity that makes you feel at ease and allows you to step away from the stresses of the day, even if only for a few minutes.

Examples of Restful Rituals

Cooking with music

For me, cooking has become a daily ritual that brings both relaxation and joy. There's something soothing about preparing a meal, focusing on the simple tasks of chopping vegetables or stirring a pot, and letting the rhythmic motions quiet my mind. I often play a relaxing playlist in the background, letting the music create an ambiance of calm. The combination of cooking and music transforms this everyday task into a therapeutic experience, helping me unwind and feel grounded.

Making a cup of tea

For others, it might be as simple as making a cup of tea. The process of boiling water, selecting your favourite tea, and waiting as it steeps can be a meditative experience. As you hold the warm cup in your hands and take that first sip, it's a moment of pause, a chance to slow down and savour the present. This small ritual can become a cherished part of your day, offering a brief respite from the demands of life.

Sitting outside at sunset

Perhaps you find peace in sitting outside at sunset, watching the sky change colours as the day transitions into night. This daily ritual can become a time of reflection, where you allow the beauty of nature to soothe your mind and body. It's a moment to disconnect from technology and reconnect with the world around you, grounding yourself in the present moment.

Morning silence

Some people find rest in beginning their day with a few moments of silence. Before the busyness of the day begins, taking a few minutes to sit quietly, breathe deeply, and set an intention for the day can create a sense of calm that carries through the hours ahead. This simple practice can help you start your day with a clear mind and a peaceful heart.

Incorporating daily rituals like these into your life can have a profound impact on your overall well-being. They serve as anchors, helping you navigate the ups and downs of life with greater ease. These moments of rest don't require much effort or take up much time, but they can significantly reduce stress and increase your sense of inner peace.

Moreover, daily rituals remind you to prioritise self-care, even in small ways. They create a rhythm in your day that helps you stay connected to yourself, ensuring that you take regular breaks to recharge your mind, body, and spirit. Over time, these rituals can become a source of strength and resilience, helping you face life's challenges with a calmer, more centred approach.

Creating Your Own Rituals

To create your own daily rituals for rest, start by identifying activities that bring you comfort and joy. Think about what helps you feel at ease, whether it's a hobby, a sensory experience, or a simple task, and jot them down in your notebook. Then, find a way to incorporate these activities into your daily routine, ideally at a consistent time each day.

Remember, the goal is not to add more to your to-do list but to find small, manageable ways to rest and recharge. Your rituals should feel natural and enjoyable, not forced or burdensome. As you integrate these practices into your life, you'll likely find that they become cherished moments that you look forward to, moments that provide a sense of calm and restoration in your busy day.

In essence, daily rituals are about creating intentional spaces for rest in your life. They are small acts of self-care that, over time, can have a big impact on your well-being. Whether it's through cooking, making tea, enjoying nature, or sitting in silence, these rituals offer a pathway to deeper rest and a more peaceful existence.

Reflect: A Journey Within

"The unexamined life is not worth living."

Socrates (c. 470–399 BC)
Classical Greek philosopher

During my time of rest at home in Botswana, I embarked on a journey of reflection, a deep and necessary exploration of myself and the circumstances I found myself in, having been robbed of thousands of euros in pursuit of my dream. The situation I faced was difficult, but I knew that if I wanted to regain control of my thoughts, emotions, and actions, I needed to look beyond the immediate challenges. I had to go deeper, to examine the underlying patterns and beliefs that no longer served me, and ultimately, to move on from the loss I had experienced.

Reflection is more than a pause; it is a powerful tool for personal growth and rejuvenation. When you take the time to look inward, you uncover insights about yourself that can guide you towards a more fulfilling life. Yet, in the hustle and bustle of daily existence, it's easy to lose sight of this inner journey, becoming so absorbed in the routine that you forget to ask the deeper questions. That's why, periodically, it's essential to step back and reflect on where you are and where you want to be.

Whether you're feeling stuck, unhappy, or even content with life as it is, self-reflection offers an opportunity to reassess and realign with your true self. It's a chance to pause, to listen to your inner voice, and to make conscious choices about the direction you want to take. Even in times of satisfaction, reflection helps maintain and deepen your sense of peace and happiness, ensuring that you continue to grow and evolve.

Action Steps

Steps for Self-Reflection

Self-reflection doesn't have to be a complicated process. It begins with simple questions that prompt you to pay attention to your immediate situation. These questions help you to live more fully in the present moment, rather than being consumed by worries about the future or regrets about the past.

Here's how you can start:

1. **How am I feeling at this moment?** Begin by tuning into your emotions. What are you feeling right now? Joy, sadness, frustration, contentment? Recognising your current emotional state is the first step towards understanding your inner world.
2. **Why am I experiencing these emotions?** Dig deeper into the emotions you've identified. What's causing them? Is it something external, a situation or interaction? Or is it something internal, such as thoughts, memories, or beliefs? Understanding the root of your emotions can provide clarity and insight.
3. **What is going well in my life?** Shifting your focus to the positives can be incredibly empowering. What are the things that are working in your life right now? It could be relationships, career, personal growth, or even small daily routines that bring you joy. Acknowledging these positives helps reinforce gratitude and satisfaction.
4. **What would I change in my life?** Reflect on the areas of your life that may not be aligning with your values or desires. What aspects do you wish to change? This might be about setting new goals, making lifestyle adjustments, or altering your mindset. Identifying these areas is the first step towards making meaningful changes.
5. **What is my greatest achievement?** Take a moment to celebrate your successes. What are you most proud of? Reflecting on your achievements, big or small, reinforces a sense of accomplishment and motivates you to continue pursuing your goals.
6. **What am I thankful for?** Gratitude (which I will delve deeply into later on) is a powerful tool for shifting your perspective. What are the things in your life that you are truly thankful for? This could be people,

opportunities, experiences, or even challenges that have taught you valuable lessons. Fostering gratitude helps you focus on the abundance in your life rather than its shortcomings.

The ultimate goal of reflection is to reconnect with yourself, to gain a clearer understanding of who you are, and to rejuvenate your soul. Life is a constant journey, and without regular reflection, it's easy to lose direction. By taking the time to reflect, you can ensure that your actions and decisions are aligned with your true self, leading to a more meaningful and fulfilling life.

As you navigate your own journey of self-reflection, remember that this process is ongoing. It is not about achieving a final state of perfection but about continuously learning, growing, and evolving. Whether you are facing challenges or enjoying a period of contentment, reflection will always be a valuable tool for maintaining peace, happiness, and a sense of purpose.

So, take a deep breath, pause, and ask yourself these questions and write the answers in your notebook. Allow yourself the time and space to explore your inner world. You may be surprised by what you discover, and how these insights can guide you towards a brighter, more fulfilling future.

Moreover, think deeply on where you are in life. This can help you determine if there are certain things you want to work towards, and it also gives you a chance to feel grateful for what you have and to let go of what you don't.

Setting Goals

1. Think About Your Future and Set Realistic Goals

Goal setting is more than a process; it's a fundamental aspect of achieving success and abundance in life. It is a powerful process for thinking about your ideal future and for motivating yourself to turn your vision of this future into reality. By clearly defining what you want, creating a plan to achieve it, and committing to the necessary actions, you turn abstract ideas into tangible outcomes. Whether you're aiming for personal growth, professional success, or lifestyle changes, setting clear and actionable goals is essential to making progress.

Think of this metaphor: goal setting is like planting a seed in fertile soil. With careful planning and nurturing, that tiny seed, which is your goal, begins to sprout and grow. Each small action you take is like watering and tending to the seedling, helping it to develop roots and reach towards the sun. Over time, with patience and perseverance, that seed transforms into a thriving tree, bearing the fruits of your hard work and dedication. Just as you need to envision the tree long before it grows, it is vital to clearly see your goal and commit to the daily care needed to make it a reality.

Call to Action

Begin by envisioning what you want to achieve. This could be related to your career, personal life, health, or any other area. Think about where you want to be in the future and define what success looks like for you. Ensure that your goals are **SMART**:

- **Specific:** Clearly define what you want to accomplish.
- **Measurable:** Determine how you will measure progress and know when the goal is achieved.

- **Achievable:** Make sure your goal is realistic and attainable within your current resources and constraints.
- **Relevant:** Ensure the goal is aligned with your broader life goals and values.
- **Time-bound:** Set a deadline or time frame for achieving the goal.

Here is an example of a SMART goal I set for myself:

As a nurse, I began to envision a different future for myself, one that was free from the demanding night shifts at the hospital. I saw myself stepping into a new role, one that allowed me to reclaim my days and restore balance to my life. In my mind's eye, I pictured the crisp morning air as I prepared for work, no longer feeling the weight of exhaustion from a long night. Instead of scrubs, I imagined myself dressing in tailored, professional attire, a sleek blouse paired with perfectly pressed trousers or a smart skirt, my hair neatly styled, and a touch of make-up to highlight my features.

I would leave my home as the sun rose, a cup of coffee in hand, with time to savour it rather than gulping it down between patient rounds. The commute to work was no longer a blur of darkness and empty streets but a peaceful drive bathed in the golden glow of the morning light. As I arrived at my new office, I could feel the sense of calm and control that came with a nine-to-five schedule, knowing that my evenings were my own to spend and pursue hobbies, or simply relax.

Walking into the office, I envisioned the soft hum of computers and the steady rhythm of a routine that didn't involve rushing to respond to emergencies or managing the chaos of a busy ward. My desk was organised, my day planned out with meetings and tasks that allowed me to use my nursing knowledge in a different, more structured way. I saw myself sitting comfortably in a modern, ergonomic chair, working on projects that challenged me intellectually but didn't drain me physically.

Gone were the fluorescent lights and the constant beeping of monitors; instead, I was surrounded by natural light streaming through the windows and the quiet chatter of colleagues discussing their latest projects. My lunch breaks were no longer hurried affairs but leisurely moments where I could step outside, enjoy the sunshine, and return to work refreshed.

The vision was clear: I was no longer a nurse bound to the hospital's relentless schedule. I had transitioned to a role where I could bring my expertise to the table in a different capacity, one that allowed me to maintain a healthier work-life balance. This was the life I saw for myself, one filled with purpose, but also with the time and energy to enjoy all the other aspects of life that had been on hold for so long.

Satisfied with this vision, I then took my pen and outlined my SMART goal as follows:

Specific: I will transition from my current nursing role, which involves demanding night shifts, to a new position that allows for a regular nine-to-five schedule. This new role will enable me to use my nursing expertise in a more structured, office-based environment, where I can maintain a healthier work-life balance.

Measurable: I will apply to at least five relevant job opportunities that align with my vision of a daytime schedule and a professional setting. I will also update my résumé and LinkedIn profile to reflect my qualifications and career aspirations.

Achievable: I will leverage my nursing experience and skills to explore roles in healthcare administration, case management, or a related field that offers regular working hours. To prepare for this transition, I will research potential job openings, network with professionals in my desired field, and possibly take an online course or certification to enhance my qualifications.

Relevant: This goal is directly aligned with my desire to improve my work-life balance and well-being by moving away from the physical and emotional demands of night shifts in a hospital setting. It supports my long-term vision of a career that provides fulfilment while also allowing time for personal pursuits and self-care.

Time-bound: I will complete this transition within the next six months. During this time, I will aim to secure a new position that fits my criteria and begin my new role by the start of the next quarter.

2. Break Down Goals into Smaller Steps

Large goals can feel overwhelming, so break them down into smaller, more manageable tasks. Each smaller step should be a goal in itself, contributing to the overall objective.

3. Create an Action Plan

Develop a detailed action plan that outlines the specific steps you need to take to achieve your goal. Include deadlines for each step and allocate resources as needed.

4. Monitor and Adjust

Regularly review your progress towards your goals. If you encounter obstacles, be flexible and willing to adjust your plan. This might involve refining your goals, changing your approach, or extending your timeline.

5. Celebrate Achievements

Acknowledge and celebrate each milestone you achieve. This not only boosts your morale but also reinforces your commitment to your goals.

Common Pitfalls in Goal Setting

1. **Setting Vague Goals**

   Goals that are not specific can lead to confusion and lack of direction. Ensure that your goals are clear and well-defined.

2. **Lack of Realism**

   Setting goals that are too ambitious or unrealistic can lead to frustration and burnout. Be honest about your capabilities and resources when setting goals.

3. **Ignoring the Importance of Flexibility**

   Life is unpredictable and circumstances can change. It's important to remain flexible and adjust your goals as needed rather than abandoning them entirely.

4. **Failure to Track Progress**

   Without tracking your progress, it's easy to lose sight of how far you've come and how much further you need to go. Regularly monitor your progress to stay motivated and on course.

5. **Not Setting Time Frames**

   Without a deadline, there's no sense of urgency. Time frames help create a sense of priority and prevent procrastination.

Step Away From Distractions

In a world where we are constantly bombarded with information and entertainment from our devices, it can be challenging to step away from these distractions. However, unplugging from electronics, even for a short period, allows us to reconnect with ourselves. The quietness that comes from being disconnected provides a space for us to listen to our thoughts, process our emotions, and even face the discomfort of boredom. Often seen as a negative state, boredom can be a powerful catalyst for creativity and introspection. When we are not constantly occupied with external stimuli, our minds have the freedom to wander, explore new ideas, and reflect on our inner experiences. This process of self-reflection is crucial for your personal growth, helping you to understand your desires, fears, and motivations more deeply.

Connect with Nature

Nature offers a sanctuary from the artificial environments we inhabit most of the time. When you spend time in nature, you are reminded of the simplicity and beauty of the world around us. The rustling of leaves, the chirping of birds, the feeling of the wind on our skin: all these sensory experiences ground you in the present moment and offer a profound sense of peace. Nature's rhythms, like the changing seasons or the flow of a river, can also teach us important lessons about life's natural cycles and the importance of patience and resilience. Breathing in fresh air and immersing ourselves in natural surroundings revitalises not only our bodies but also our minds and spirits. The opportunity to reflect during a walk in nature can lead to bursts of creative thinking, as the peaceful environment allows our thoughts to flow freely. This connection with nature is not just about physical health but also about nurturing our mental and emotional well-being, reminding us of our place in the larger world and helping us cultivate a sense of gratitude and contentment.

Restart: Rise Stronger And Wiser

Life can be overwhelming when everything seems to go wrong, threatening to knock you down and blinding you to the possibilities ahead. In these moments, don't give up: **Restart**! This is your chance to rise stronger, wiser, and ready to begin your journey anew.

Restarting after a period of rest and reflection offers a powerful opportunity to realign with your true self, apply the lessons you've learned, and approach your goals with renewed vigour. After my own period of rest and reflection in Botswana, I had to figure out how to restart my life, bringing more energy, satisfaction, joy, and gratitude into each day. One crucial lesson I learned is this: it's **never too late** to restart.

Top Tips

Here are a few strategies that helped me, and I believe they can help you too.

1. **Acknowledge the Value of Rest**

   Rest is often undervalued in our fast-paced world, yet it's one of the most critical components of long-term success. Taking time to rest isn't simply about physical recovery; it's also about giving your mind the space to process emotions, reflect on experiences, and gain new insights. When you rest, you allow your body to heal and your mind to reorganise and clarify your thoughts. This period of downtime can be incredibly rejuvenating, offering you a fresh perspective and renewed energy to tackle your goals. Rest is not a sign of weakness or defeat; it's a strategic pause that prepares you for the challenges ahead.

2. **Revisit Your Goals and Values**

   As time passes, our circumstances, experiences, and even our desires evolve. That's why it's crucial to periodically revisit your goals and values. What might have been important to you a year ago may no longer hold the same significance. Reassessing your goals ensures that they align with your current life situation and aspirations. For instance, when I revisited my goal of relocating, I realised that despite the challenges, my desire to move was still strong. This reflection helped me confirm that my goal was still relevant and worth pursuing. By trusting your instincts and being honest with yourself, you can ensure that your actions are in harmony with your true desires.

3. **Create a Restart Plan**

   A restart plan is your roadmap for moving forward. It's about letting go of the past, previous failures, regrets, or disappointments, and focusing on what lies ahead. A fresh perspective is essential for this. When I lost a significant amount of money due to a fraudulent agency, I was devastated. However, my mother's wise advice to move on helped me shift my focus from what I had lost, to what I could gain in the future. Creating a restart plan involves setting new, realistic goals, identifying the steps needed to achieve them, and maintaining a positive mindset. It's about transforming setbacks into set-ups for a better future.

4. **Rebuild Momentum**

   Starting small is key to rebuilding momentum. After a setback, it's tempting to try and catch up quickly, but this approach can lead to burnout. Instead, set small, achievable goals that gradually build your confidence and productivity. For example, if you're restarting a fitness routine, begin with short, manageable workouts rather than jumping into intense sessions. Each small victory will boost your morale and create a snowball effect, making it easier to tackle larger challenges as you progress. Momentum builds gradually, so be patient and consistent.

5. **Leverage Lessons Learned**

   One of the most valuable outcomes of any challenging period is the lessons you learn. These insights are the key to avoiding past mistakes and improving your future efforts. Reflect on what worked well before and what didn't and use this knowledge to refine your strategies. For instance, if stress was a major factor in your previous burnout, you might now prioritise setting boundaries or incorporating regular self-care practices into your routine. By understanding the root causes of your challenges, you can make informed decisions that lead to more sustainable success.

6. **Stay Inspired and Celebrate Achievements**

   Inspiration is the fuel that keeps you moving forward, especially during challenging times. Find sources of inspiration that resonate with you, whether it's reading motivational books, surrounding yourself with supportive people, or setting personal rewards for milestones achieved. Celebrating your achievements, no matter how small, is equally important. This practice not only boosts your motivation but also reinforces your self-belief. Each celebration is a reminder that you're making progress, and helps sustain your energy and enthusiasm as you continue on your path.

Remember, restarting isn't a setback, it's a new beginning. It's an opportunity to realign with your true self, re-energise your efforts, and re-emerge stronger than before. Embrace the restart as a chance to apply the wisdom you've gained, set fresh goals, and approach your journey with renewed passion. With the right mindset and strategies in place, a restart can be the launchpad for your greatest achievements.

The mindset of persevering through tough times, of keeping on, even when the road seems steep, is a vital one to cultivate. In the next chapter, we'll dive into how you can develop this resilient mindset. But for now, remember this: when you're facing difficulties or setbacks and the weight feels overwhelming, allow yourself to **Rest, Reflect, and Restart**. These moments of pause are not signs of defeat; they are necessary steps to reassess your goals, realign your path, and renew your energy.

But above all, don't lose sight of the importance of pushing forward. Even when the odds seem stacked against you, keep moving forward with hope. Rest and reflection can guide you, and restarting gives you a fresh perspective, but it's your determination to keep going that will ultimately lead you to success. I faced my own challenges, and I didn't let them define me or my goals. Instead, I chose to keep on keeping on, driven by hope. And you can too.

PEARLS OF WISDOM

Keep On Keeping On Through Hardship

The phrase "keep on keeping on" connotes the importance of persistence in the face of difficulties. Life will inevitably present challenges, but continuing to move forward, even when the road is tough, is essential to achieving your goals and eventually your success. Persistence is about enduring and outlasting the challenges.

Life's Journey Is Full of Tests

The analogy of a road trip represents life's journey filled with potholes, storms, and setbacks. Life tests our resolve, but these challenges are part of the journey, not the destination. Knowing that trials will come helps prepare you mentally to face them with strength and resilience.

Your Why Is Your Compass

Understanding your why, the purpose or goal that drives you, is a crucial element in enduring life's hardships. Just like a compass keeping a traveller on course, your reason for pursuing your dreams will help guide you through life's storms and uncertainties.

Adversity Builds Character

Overcoming challenges doesn't only get you to the other side; rather, it shapes who you are. The ability to push through adversity helps develop resilience, determination, and strength of character. These qualities are not just important for reaching your goals; they become part of who you are.

The Power of Reflecting on Your Journey

Reflecting on your challenges helps you understand your own strength and capacity for growth. By looking back on moments where you felt "tangled up in the blue" but continued to press forward, you gain insight into your resilience and ability to persevere.

The Importance of Support Systems

The chapter touches on the role that loved ones play during difficult times, as evidenced by my mother offering wisdom during a moment of crisis. Having a support system, whether it's family, friends, or mentors, can provide encouragement and clarity when challenges seem overwhelming.

Pause, Reflect, and Restart

The decision to pause, return home, and restart the journey signifies the importance of reflection and taking breaks when necessary. Sometimes persistence doesn't mean charging forward without stopping; it can also mean stepping back to reassess, gather strength, and then resume with renewed energy.

Mistakes and Setbacks Don't Define You

The experience of being swindled by a fraudulent agency was devastating, but it didn't define my destiny. Mistakes, failures, and setbacks are part of the process, but they don't have to derail your long-term vision. It's how you respond to those setbacks that matters.

Your Purpose Is Worth the Struggle

The belief that my why was worth the challenges I faced is a powerful reminder. When you believe that your goals and dreams are worthwhile, it becomes easier to endure the struggles along the way. This belief can provide motivation when everything else seems to be falling apart.

Growth Through Challenges, Not Just Survival

Persistence is not just about surviving hardships; it's about growing through them. The challenges you face are not simply obstacles to overcome, but are opportunities for personal growth. Learning from adversity and becoming stronger through each trial is key to achieving long-term success.

PART 3

HOPE

"We must accept finite disappointment, but never lose infinite hope."

Martin Luther King Jr. (1929–1968)
American civil rights leader and minister

LET ME SHARE A STORY that captures the essence of hope.[16]

Once upon a time, there was a young farmer named Ramu who faced overwhelming challenges. His land, once fertile, had been ravaged by drought, leaving it barren and lifeless. Despite the despair that hung over his land, Ramu didn't lose hope. He gathered the few seeds he had left and planted them in the dry, cracked soil. With unwavering faith, he watered them and tended to them with care and perseverance. To his amazement, tiny sprouts began to emerge, eventually blossoming into a bountiful harvest.

Ramu's story teaches us that even in the darkest times, hope can bloom if we remain determined and work hard.

This story brings me back to a period of rest and reflection when I was home in Botswana. My mother, in her gentle wisdom, often reminded me, "Have hope; everything will fall into place. It will be okay." At that moment, I didn't fully grasp the power of hope until I came across a definition by the American Psychological Association. They define hope as *"the expectation that one will have positive experiences or that a potentially threatening or negative situation will not materialize or will ultimately result in a favourable state of affairs."*

At some point in our lives, we've all experienced that sinking feeling of losing hope. The pandemic, for instance, eroded many people's sense of hope. So how do you stay hopeful when everything seems to be falling apart? There's no single formula, but I'll share with you the steps that helped me cultivate hope amid challenges.

My Story

Before I share those steps, let me continue with my story.

After a period of rest and reflection in Botswana, I decided to return to Ireland to pursue my dreams. Many people might have given up at this point, especially after facing obstacles. The questions of doubt – "What if I fail again?" and "What if I'm not meant to start a new life abroad?" – could have easily taken over, allowing fear and hopelessness to set in.

But instead of giving up, I chose to act like Ramu, the young farmer. I gathered the little I had left, packed my bags, and boarded a flight back to Ireland. I didn't know what the future held for me, but I carried hope with me, a new slate, a fresh start, and the promise of new adventures.

One cold, rainy evening, as doubts started to creep in, I decided to explore the possibility of registering as a nurse in Ireland. The next morning, I took a bus to the nursing board with all my qualifications in hand. A few days later, I received an application package in the mail. I immediately began the process, and months later, I received a letter confirming my eligibility to register as a nurse in Ireland.

I called home to share the good news with my mother, thinking this was the beginning of a smooth road ahead. But little did I know that another challenge awaited me. The letter of eligibility was valid for only one year, and within that year, I needed to find a registered care body or hospital to sponsor my nursing adaptation, a six-week internship required for all nurses trained overseas. The thought of finally getting registered kept me hopeful, and I began applying for internships. But rejection after rejection came, and the year quickly slipped by.

As the deadline loomed, I reached out to the Overseas Adaptation Programme Coordinator, who informed me that even if I found a sponsor within the year, the intake for 2013 was full. The next intake wouldn't be until 2015, a long waiting period. Despite this setback, the thought of giving up never crossed my mind.

I contacted the Nursing Board to request an extension on my eligibility letter. I sent emails, made phone calls, and waited. But no response came. I began to feel hopeless, but I held on to my mother's words: "Keep your faith; do not lose hope."

I'm sure you've faced rejection at some point in your life, and perhaps you wanted to give up. You may have lost hope. But how do you stay hopeful when things aren't going your way?

How do you cultivate hope?

Living Your Values

Values are the foundation of our decisions and actions, guiding us through life's challenges and uncertainties. They represent what matters most to us and serve as a compass when navigating difficult situations. Living in alignment with your values fosters a sense of authenticity and purpose, which fuels hope and resilience, especially during trying times.

Values are deeply held beliefs that define who we are and what we stand for. They come from various influences, such as upbringing, culture, and personal experiences. These values dictate the standards we set for ourselves and how we evaluate right from wrong, good from bad. When our actions align with these values, we feel more fulfilled and connected to our true selves. When there's a misalignment, we experience discomfort and dissatisfaction, a sense that something essential is missing.

Aligning your goals with your values makes them more meaningful and fulfilling. When your objectives reflect what matters most to you, it becomes easier to stay motivated and hopeful. This alignment allows you to act in ways that are goal-oriented, but also deeply satisfying, creating a life that feels purposeful and authentic.

My five core values – integrity, determination, excellence, kindness, and honesty – are my compass. They shape my decisions and actions every day:

1. **Integrity:** Integrity is about being true to yourself and others, making decisions that reflect your principles. In both my personal and professional life, I refuse to compromise my ethical standards, even when it would be easier to do so. True success, in my view, is built on trust, respect, and transparency.
2. **Determination:** The path of success is often filled with obstacles, and determination is what keeps me moving forward. When I made the bold decision to leave my home country and pursue a different career, I faced numerous setbacks. Yet, my determination pushed me through, helping me break down my goals into manageable tasks and persist until I succeeded.
3. **Excellence:** Excellence means striving to be the best version of myself, continuously improving in both personal and professional arenas. I aim high and work diligently to meet my own standards, recognising that

excellence is not about perfection but about consistent progress.

4. **Kindness:** Treating others with kindness and empathy fosters positive connections and a supportive environment. I make it a priority to be kind, whether in my interactions with family, friends, colleagues, or strangers. This creates a ripple effect, encouraging hope and resilience in myself and those around me.
5. **Honesty:** Being truthful is essential in building trust. Honesty drives my communication, ensuring clarity and understanding in both personal and professional relationships. It allows me to maintain authentic and meaningful connections, which is vital for fostering hope and mutual support.

Aligning your goals with your values starts with self-reflection. Ask yourself, "What are my core principles? What do I stand for?" Think about moments in your life where you felt a deep sense of fulfilment – these instances often reflect your true values. Once you've identified your values, jot them down in your notebook.

Next, you need to assess your goals. Do they align with what matters most to you? If not, adjust your goals so that they are in sync with your values. When your goals reflect your values, they become more than just tasks; they become an expression of who you are. This makes it easier to stay motivated, even when faced with obstacles, because your actions are rooted in authenticity. You'll also experience a deeper sense of satisfaction as your progress feels like it is aligned with your purpose.

Cultivating a Growth Mindset

A growth mindset is essential for nurturing hope, especially during challenging times. Popularised by Carol Dweck, the concept of a growth mindset revolves around the belief that our abilities can be developed through dedication, effort, and persistence. It stands in contrast to a fixed mindset, where individuals believe their talents and intelligence are static, often leading to a fear of failure and avoidance of challenges.

A fixed mindset limits your potential. It leads to avoiding challenges, fearing failure, and sticking to what's comfortable. In contrast, a growth mindset embraces challenges and views failure as an opportunity for growth. This perspective fosters resilience and optimism, two key ingredients for hope. When you believe in your ability to grow, you're more likely to stay motivated, even when things aren't going your way.

Here's a quick comparison:

Fixed Mindset	Growth Mindset
• Avoids challenges	• Embraces challenges
• It is too hard	• I can train my brain
• Expect reward without effort	• Effort is a path to mastery
• Ignore feedback	• Learn from feedback
• Threatened by success of other	• Inspired by success of others
• Intelligence is static	• Intelligence can be developed

One of the hallmarks of a growth mindset is the willingness to face challenges head-on. When I left my secure nursing career to pursue a new path, I faced uncertainty and fear of failure. However, instead of being paralysed by these feelings, I chose to embrace them as opportunities for growth. I reminded myself that every setback was a stepping stone, a lesson in resilience, and a chance to grow stronger. In a growth mindset, failure isn't a reflection of your worth; it's an opportunity to learn. Every time I faced a setback, whether in my personal life or professional career, I viewed it as a lesson. Failure can be disheartening, but with a growth mindset, it becomes a stepping stone towards future success.

Research has shown that adopting a growth mindset can lead to lower levels of stress and anxiety, as well as higher levels of psychological well-being. A study titled 'Growth mindsets of anxiety: Do the benefits to individual flourishing come with societal costs?' by psychologist Hoyt et al. (2023)[17] demonstrated that individuals with a growth mindset are more likely to thrive in stressful situations because they view these challenges as opportunities to learn and grow.

By cultivating a growth mindset, you open yourself up to new possibilities and develop the resilience needed to navigate difficult times. Hope thrives when you believe that you have the capacity to grow and improve, no matter the obstacles in your way.

Top Tips

How to Develop a Growth Mindset

1. **Embrace Challenges:** Don't shy away from difficult tasks. Instead, see them as opportunities to learn and grow.
2. **View Failure as a Learning Opportunity:** Every mistake is a lesson in disguise. Reflect on what you can learn from your failures and use those insights to move forward.
3. **Celebrate Effort Over Success:** Focus on the process, not just the outcome. When you value effort, you develop a love for learning and a perseverance that will keep hope alive, even in tough times.
4. **Learn From Feedback:** Be open to constructive criticism. Use feedback to improve yourself rather than viewing it as a personal attack.

When paired with hope, a growth mindset can transform how you approach life. It fosters resilience, encourages optimism, and fuels your belief that your goals are attainable, even in the face of setbacks.

The Power of Kindness

"I've learned that people will forget what you said, people will forget what you did, but people will never forget how you made them feel."

Maya Angelou (1928–2014)
American poet, memoirist, and civil rights activist

This quote perfectly captures the essence of human connection. Acts of kindness, whether grand or small, leave lasting impressions that can uplift and inspire others in ways we may never fully understand.

Oprah Winfrey shared a powerful story from 1998 that illustrates this beautifully[18]. During her infamous trial over remarks she made about eating burgers, representatives of the beef industry accused her of trying to damage their business. Oprah felt isolated and under attack, convinced that everyone was rooting against her. Then, one morning, a woman approached her through a fence separating the courthouse from the sidewalk. She handed Oprah a matchbook with a simple message inside: "Hang in there. I am praying for you."

Oprah never knew the woman's name, nor did she ever see her again, but that small act of kindness stayed with her. It reminded her that even in the darkest moments, we are never truly alone.

This story of kindness reminded me of a similar experience in my own life, one that I would like to share with you.

My Story

Amidst the disappointments, obstacles, and feelings of darkness that seemed to surround me, I held on to a small glimmer of hope that somehow, things would turn around. While trying to regain my footing, I found a job as a healthcare assistant, as already mentioned. It was in this role that I met Mary, a woman in her seventies, who turned out to be an angel in disguise.

From the moment we met, Mary and I connected on a deep level. Her presence in my life became a source of comfort and positivity, diverting my mind from the doubts and fears that had begun to creep in about my decision to relocate abroad. Mary's words, often spoken with warmth and sincerity, echoed in my heart: "Enjoy life knowing you can reach your potential and be who you want to be. I'm praying for you that things work out in Ireland."

Those words were like a lifeline, reminding me of the stranger's message to Oprah during her trial. Mary became more than a patient to me; she became a friend, an inspiration, and a mother figure. We shared our deepest secrets, stories, and emotions, tears of both joy and sadness. We celebrated Easter, birthdays, and even Christmas together. Our bond grew stronger with each passing day, rooted in a shared passion for music.

Mary was a pianist, and I had always dreamt of playing the guitar. When I shared this with her, she encouraged me without hesitation. "Do it, Pearl! You're a woman of many talents, integrity, and values. There's no reason why you can't," she reassured me. Her words filled my eyes with tears; tears of disbelief, hope, sadness, joy, and even confusion. How do you meet such beautiful souls in life who fill your heart with hope and help you forget the hurdles you face?

Inspired by Mary's kindness and encouragement, I began music lessons two weeks later. I learned to play the guitar, and with each strum, I started to believe in myself again. Mary would listen to me play, her eyes lighting up with joy as I sang for her. Those moments became a beacon of light during my time as her carer, even as I continued to navigate the prolonged process of obtaining my nursing registration.

Mary's kindness and encouragement not only helped me rediscover my passion, but also restored my hope during a challenging time in my life. It's a reminder that even the smallest acts of kindness can have a profound impact on someone's life.

Your Turn

Here are simple acts of kindness you can try today to uplift your mood, boost your self-esteem, and connect with others.

1. **Ask someone how they are doing** and genuinely wait for their response. Sometimes, just being heard can make a world of difference.
2. **Express gratitude aloud:** Thank someone for their kindness in a heartfelt way that makes them feel truly appreciated.
3. **Hold the door for someone:** This small gesture can brighten someone's day more than you might realise.
4. **Give up your seat on a bus,** especially to someone who might need it more. It's a simple way to show consideration and care.
5. **Offer to make a cup of tea or coffee for someone at work:** A thoughtful act that can warm both your hearts.
6. **Leave an encouraging note:** Tuck a positive message where someone will find it, like on a co-worker's desk or inside a library book. It's a surprise that can make someone's day.
7. **Compliment a stranger:** A genuine compliment can lift someone's spirits and remind them of their worth.
8. **Help someone carry their groceries:** Whether it's a neighbour or a stranger, lending a hand with heavy bags shows you care.
9. **Donate items you no longer need:** Clothes, books, or household items that you don't use anymore can be treasures for someone else.
10. **Send a thoughtful text:** Reach out to a friend or family member to let them know you're thinking of them. A simple "How are you?" or "I appreciate you" can mean a lot.

11. **Pick up litter:** Whether it's in your neighbourhood or at a park, taking a moment to clean up can make your environment better for everyone.
12. **Share a smile:** It's the easiest and quickest way to spread positivity. A smile can be contagious and brighten someone's day.

These small acts of kindness not only make others feel valued but also enrich your own life, creating a ripple effect of positivity in the world around you. So why not start today? Your simple gesture could be the highlight of someone's day.

PEARLS OF WISDOM

Values Anchor Us in Uncertain Times

When life feels overwhelming, holding onto core values like kindness and hope provides direction, helping us stay grounded and resilient.

Kindness Reflects Your Values

The way you treat others speaks volumes about your personal values. Leading with kindness is a daily commitment to live with integrity and compassion.

Hope Grows From a Strong Value System

Believing in something bigger than yourself, whether it's faith, love, or the potential for a better future, fosters a deep sense of hope that carries you through difficult times.

Kindness Is an Expression of Inner Strength

It takes courage to be kind in a harsh world. By embodying kindness, you're living out your values, showing strength, and creating positive change.

Your Values Shape Your Hope for the Future

What you value today shapes the hope you carry for tomorrow. If you value community, fairness, or love, you'll naturally envision a world filled with those qualities.

Kindness Leads to Lasting Fulfilment

Temporary success may bring happiness, but living in alignment with your values, especially kindness, brings long-term fulfilment and peace.

Hope Is the Heartbeat of Your Values

Hope fuels your values, giving them life and purpose. Without hope, values like kindness, generosity, and empathy would be harder to sustain.

Values-Driven Kindness Builds Trust

When your kindness comes from a place of true values, it's authentic and trustworthy. People feel safe and valued around those who live by their principles.

Hope Requires Courage

Having hope in challenging times is an act of courage that draws on your deepest values. It's about believing in possibilities, even when they aren't visible yet.

Your Values Inspire Others to Hope

When you live by values such as kindness, honesty, and empathy, you inspire others to have hope in humanity and in the possibility of a better world.

PART 4

GRIEF

"Grief is the price we pay for love".

Queen Elizabeth II (1926–2022)
Queen of the United Kingdom

GRIEF IS AN UNAVOIDABLE part of the human experience, touching us all in different ways. It can stem from a variety of losses, whether it's the death of a loved one, the end of a relationship, the loss of a job, or the sudden upheaval of life as we know it. In their 2024 study, 'Grief Reactions and Prolonged Grief Disorder', Mughal et al.[19] discuss grief as a natural and individualised response to loss, which can manifest as emotional distress, suffering, and even negative health outcomes. But while grief is universal, how we cope with it is deeply personal.

In our lives, many of us have already faced grief, and we will all encounter it at some point. The real challenge lies in how we manage to navigate through it. Mughal and his colleagues concluded that grief can bring symptoms like sadness, anger, stress, insomnia, depression, anxiety, and even physical conditions such as myocardial infarctions, particularly in those with pre-existing heart issues. These findings raise important questions: How do we cope with grief? What strategies can we use to overcome it?

But before we explore the science and strategies, I'd like to share my personal journey through grief, a story that still echoes in my heart today.

My Story

In June 2015, I received life-changing news. I had been offered a sponsorship to begin my long-awaited nursing internship in Ireland! It was a moment of triumph for me, my family, and my dear friend Mary, whom I had cared for. Yet, amid the excitement, the thought of leaving Mary behind was heart-wrenching. We spent our last days together, cherishing every moment before I departed to pursue my career.

What followed was a year filled with both personal and professional challenges, as the road to my dreams became increasingly difficult. Days into my internship, I received distressing news: my mother had fallen seriously ill. Balancing the demands of my internship with the emotional turmoil of my mother's declining health was overwhelming. But my mother, ever the pillar of strength, urged me to stay in Ireland and complete my training. Despite her condition worsening, she insisted that I focus on my future.

Her words weighed heavily on me, but I clung to them, finding solace in my faith and the wisdom of those who had guided me. I continued my internship, concealing my inner struggles from my colleagues until the burden became too great. When I finally confided in my nursing managers, they granted me permission to return home for two weeks to be with my mother. It was a bittersweet reunion. The reality of her deteriorating condition, compounded by the poor medical care she received, broke my heart.

Despite everything, she encouraged me to return to Ireland and complete my internship. With a heavy heart, I obeyed, knowing it was what she wanted.

The final days of my internship were agonising. My mother's condition continued to worsen, and the thought of losing her consumed me. When I finally completed my internship, I booked a flight home, hoping to be by her side in her final moments. But fate had other plans: my mother passed away just hours after I made the arrangements.

The news shattered me. Alone in my apartment in Ireland, I felt the weight of the world on my shoulders. I hastily rescheduled my flight and prepared for the long journey home, knowing that nothing could truly prepare me for what awaited.

The days leading up to my mother's funeral were surreal. I struggled to process the loss, and the emotional toll was immense. At the funeral, I took on the responsibility of ensuring my mother looked peaceful, even fixing her make-up myself. I delivered her eulogy, speaking of her love, wisdom, and the impact she had on all who knew her. It was a day of immense sorrow, but also of profound love and respect for a woman who had given me so much.

As if the loss of my mother wasn't enough, I soon learned of the tragic death of a beloved mentor, Mr Shakes, who had supported me throughout my nursing education. His passing, so soon after my mother's, left me reeling. And then, days later, another blow: Mary, my dear friend in Ireland, had passed away. The grief was unbearable, and I returned to Ireland with a heavy heart, feeling utterly lost.

Grief consumed me in the months that followed. I struggled with sleepless nights, anxiety, and a deep sense of isolation. The pain of losing my mother, mentor, and friend in such a short time span was overwhelming. I withdrew from activities I once enjoyed and found it difficult to balance work and school. Eventually, I made the difficult decision to take a break from college, focusing solely on work as I tried to heal.

My experience is one that many who have faced loss can relate to. Grief is a complex journey, and each of us navigates it in our own way. Through this, I learned the importance of reaching out for support, finding strength in faith, and allowing oneself the time and space to heal.

Stages of Grief

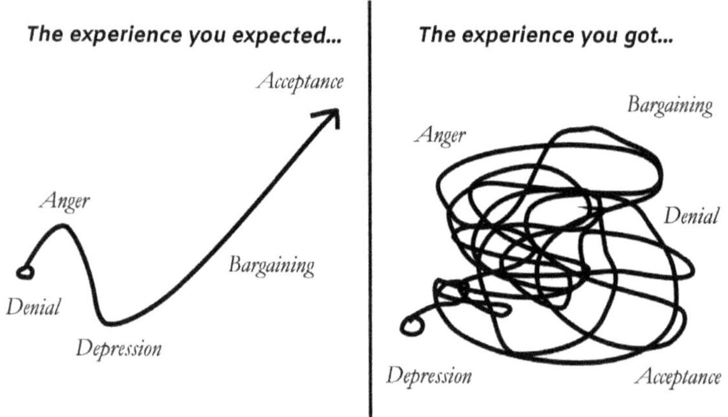

Grief is a deeply personal and often overwhelming experience that affects everyone differently. The Swiss American psychiatrist Elisabeth Kübler-Ross famously outlined the five stages of grief in her ground-breaking 1969 book, *On Death and Dying*[20]. These stages – Denial, Anger, Bargaining, Depression, and Acceptance – are often misunderstood as a linear process. However, Kübler-Ross emphasised that grief is not a straightforward journey; these stages can overlap, recur, or even occur simultaneously. Let's explore each stage more deeply, drawing on personal experiences and insights from other experts in the field.

Denial: The Numbness of Reality

Denial is often the first response to the loss of a loved one. Even when we know intellectually that someone has passed away, our heart struggles to accept the reality. This stage can manifest as a sense of disbelief, where you might find yourself expecting your loved one to walk through the door at any moment. You may feel their presence, hear their voice in a crowded room, or even pick up the phone to call them before remembering they're gone. Denial acts as a temporary shield, numbing the intensity of the loss so that we can gradually come to terms with it.

Anger: The Search for Meaning

As the numbness of denial fades, anger often takes its place. This stage is where the reality of loss begins to sink in, and it can be a turbulent time emotionally. Dr Maureen Gaffney, an Irish clinical psychologist and broadcaster, describes anger in her book *Flourishing*[21] as a natural reaction to the unfairness of loss. You might find yourself questioning why this happened to you or your loved one. Anger can be directed at the situation, at others, or even at yourself. You might think, "Why didn't I spend more time with them?" or "Why couldn't I do more to prevent this?" It's important to remember that these feelings, though painful, are a normal part of the grieving process. Anger often reflects the deep love and connection you had with the person you lost.

Bargaining: The What-Ifs

Bargaining is a stage where you might find yourself negotiating with a higher power, the universe, or even yourself. It's characterised by thoughts like, "If only I had done this differently; maybe they would still be here." According to the American Psychological Association (APA), this stage often involves irrational thoughts and what-ifs.[22] If you are religious, you might find yourself making promises to God in exchange for bringing your loved one back or preventing future loss. Clinical psychologist Dr Thea Gallagher describes this stage as being filled with anxiety, fear, and self-blame. It's a way of trying to regain control in a situation where you feel utterly powerless. You can listen to discussions on grief, including episodes that address the challenges and nuances of grieving, on *The Mind in View*[23], the podcast she co-hosts. It dives into various aspects of mental health, including a two-part series specifically about grief, where Dr Gallagher explores both personal and general experiences of loss.

Depression: The Deep Sorrow

Depression is perhaps the most well-known stage of grief, but it can also be the most misunderstood. This stage is not only about feeling sad; it's a profound sense of emptiness and despair. You might feel as though life has lost its meaning, and the future feels bleak. The pain can be so intense that it lingers for months or even years. This isn't the same as clinical depression, though the symptoms can overlap. You might withdraw from activities you once enjoyed, experience changes in sleep and appetite, or feel a deep, persistent sadness. This stage is a natural response to the magnitude of your loss and can be a necessary step in the healing process.

Acceptance: The New Normal

Acceptance is often thought of as the final stage of grief, but it doesn't mean that the pain goes away completely. Instead, it's about finding a way to live with the loss. Over time, the sharp edges of grief may soften, allowing you to remember your loved one with more fondness than pain. Acceptance doesn't mean forgetting or moving on; it means learning to live again while carrying the memory of your loved one with you. Grief, as many people describe, comes in waves. Some days are easier than others, and that's okay. Acceptance is about finding a new normal, a way to move forward while honouring the past.

It is vital to acknowledge that not everyone goes through these stages of grief as popularised. In his book, *Finding Peace When Your Heart Is in Pieces: A Step-by-Step Guide to the Other Side of Grief, Loss, and Pain,*[24] psychologist Paul Coleman highlights that some people do not go through all the stages, or in that order, and that some stages do not even apply for some.

Navigating Grief: A Personal Reflection

In my own journey through grief, these stages have been both a guide and a comfort. Losing my mother, mentor, and dear friend in such a short space of time was overwhelming. I found myself cycling through these stages, sometimes feeling them all at once. Denial came in the quiet moments when I would expect my mother's call, and anger surfaced when I questioned why I wasn't there with her more often. Bargaining filled my thoughts with what-ifs, and depression enveloped me in a deep, lingering sadness.

Yet, over time, I began to find moments of acceptance. I realised that my loved ones would want me to live fully, even without them. Their memories became a source of strength rather than sorrow, and I started to build a new life around the love and lessons they left behind.

Grief is not something you get over; it's something you go through. Each person's journey is unique, and there is no right or wrong way to grieve. Whether you're in the midst of denial, anger, bargaining, depression, or acceptance, it's important to be gentle with yourself. Grief is a testament to the love you shared, and with time, that love can help you heal.

The question now is: How do you cope with the transition of grief stages, in order to benefit your well-being, flourish, and thrive?

Coping With Grief

Grief is a profound and often overwhelming emotion that follows the loss of a loved one. Navigating this complex emotional landscape can be challenging, but certain strategies have been shown to help individuals manage their grief and begin to heal. Below are some evidence-based coping mechanisms that can support you through this difficult time.

1. **Engage in a Mind-Body Program**

   An article from Harvard Health, 'How to overcome grief's health-damaging effects',[25] noted that research led by Dr Eric Bui, Associate Director for Research at the Center for Anxiety and Traumatic Stress Disorder and Complicated Grief Program at Harvard-affiliated Massachusetts General Hospital, published online by the *American Journal of Hospice and Palliative Medicine*, found that an eight-week mind-body program significantly reduced stress in grieving older adults.[26] These programs often include elements like meditation, mindfulness, and gentle physical activity, which can help to calm the mind, reduce stress, and create a sense of inner peace. Integrating such practices into your daily routine may offer you a structured way to process your grief and restore emotional balance.

2. **Reach Out to Your Social Circle**

   During times of grief, it's natural to want to withdraw from others, but maintaining social connections is crucial for emotional support. An article by J Macfarlane on social connectivity and its role within mental health in *The British Journal of Mental Health Nursing*[27] indicates that one of the most effective ways to boost happiness is by cultivating relationships with those around you. Whether it's a weekly lunch, a coffee date, or a phone call, staying connected can provide comfort and remind you that you are not alone.

Your Turn

In your notebook, create a mind map with the names of people who make up your healthy network of social connections. They are the ones who support, energise, and enrich you. They may be:

- Family and friends
- Colleagues or managers
- Professional contacts
- Online contacts

Make a point to keep in contact with your healthy relationships and lastly, consider ways in which to stop or reduce contact with those who criticise or are unsupportive.

This approach is adopted from an article in *Greater Good Magazine* titled 'Are Some Social Ties Better Than Others?'[28] highlighted by Macfarlane (2020) in her article. This exercise is meant to help you identify and nurture relationships that bring positivity into your life.

3. **Practice Yoga, Tai Chi, or Qigong**

   Incorporating gentle physical exercises, such as yoga, tai chi, or qigong, into your routine can significantly enhance your psychological well-being. These ancient practices involve coordinated body movements, deep rhythmic breathing, and mental focus, all of which promote relaxation and emotional balance. According to clinical studies reviewed by Yeung et al. (2018),[29] tai chi and qigong have been shown to reduce symptoms of anxiety and depression, making them particularly beneficial for those coping with grief. Many online classes are tailored specifically for stress reduction and can be easily accessed from the comfort of your home.

4. **Maintain Healthy Eating Habits**

   Nutrition plays a critical role in supporting your body during times of stress and grief. The Harvard School of Public Health notes that stress often leads to cravings for comfort foods, typically processed snacks or sweets, and may cause irregular eating patterns[25]. To counter this, focus on a balanced diet rich in fruits, vegetables, lean proteins, and whole foods, while staying hydrated. These nutritious choices can bolster your resilience and provide the physical strength needed to navigate the emotional challenges of grief.

5. **Follow Good Sleep Hygiene**

   Grief can severely disrupt sleep, leaving you feeling exhausted and emotionally drained. Establishing good sleep hygiene is essential for recovery. Dr Bui emphasises the importance of going to bed at consistent hours, establishing a calming bedtime routine, and avoiding stimulants like caffeine and alcohol in the evening. A study by Szuhany et al. (2021) on 'Prolonged Grief: Course, Diagnosis, Assessment, and Treatment'[30] found that poor sleep quality is associated with more severe grief, depression, and anxiety. The British Society of Lifestyle Medicine recommends aiming for seven to nine hours of quality sleep each night to enhance your long-term physical and emotional health.

6. **Incorporate Physical Activity**

   Regular physical activity, even something as simple as a daily walk, can be incredibly effective in easing symptoms of depression, agitation, and sorrow related to grief. Exercise releases endorphins, the body's natural mood lifters, and can help you clear your mind and gain a fresh perspective. Whether you prefer walking, jogging, swimming, or cycling, find an activity that you enjoy and make it a regular part of your routine.

Coping with grief is a deeply personal journey, and there is no one-size-fits-all solution. However, by incorporating these strategies, engaging in mind-body practices, maintaining social connections, practicing gentle physical exercises, eating healthily, following good sleep hygiene, and staying active, you can support your emotional and physical well-being as you navigate the path to healing. Remember that it's okay to seek help and lean on others during this time; you don't have to go through it alone.

Self-Compassion

It's all too common for people to be their own harshest critics, especially when grappling with profound struggles like grief. When faced with pain or failure, many of us instinctively turn inward with blame and judgement, rather than offering ourselves the compassion we so readily extend to others. Professor Kristin Neff, a pioneering figure in the academic study of self-compassion, defines it as a way of relating to ourselves with kindness and understanding, particularly in moments of difficulty[31]. Instead of being harshly self-critical, self-compassion encourages us to treat ourselves with the same care we would offer a close friend.

I remember vividly how I treated myself after the death of my mother. Rather than being gentle with myself during this incredibly painful time, I was hard on myself. I blamed myself, thinking that if I had stayed with her for just a few more weeks while she was in the hospital, perhaps she wouldn't have given up on her will to live. I convinced myself that I was selfish for leaving her to pursue my own dreams. This narrative played on repeat in my mind, a relentless loop of self-reproach.

As these thoughts took hold, they began to erode my well-being. The constant self-blame and guilt led to overwhelming anxiety, persistent sadness, and sleepless nights. My eating habits deteriorated, and I lost interest in the things that once brought me joy. The weight of my self-criticism became so heavy that it crushed my motivation, to the point where I even discontinued my studies.

Looking back, I realise how much I needed self-compassion during that time, an understanding that I was doing the best I could under unimaginably difficult circumstances. But instead of offering myself kindness, I chose to dwell in guilt and self-judgement, which only deepened my pain.

Grief is complex and deeply personal, and it's natural to feel a sense of responsibility or guilt in its wake. However, self-compassion teaches us that it's okay to feel these emotions without allowing them to define us or our actions. It reminds us that suffering is part of the human experience, and that we deserve the same care and empathy we would give to someone else in our situation.

If you find yourself in a similar place, struggling with grief or another form of loss, try to recognise when you're being overly critical of yourself. Ask yourself, "Would I speak to a friend this way? What would I say to someone I care about if they were going through this?" Then, try to turn that same kindness and understanding toward yourself. It's not easy, but it's a vital step towards healing and reclaiming your sense of self amid hardship.

By practising self-compassion, you can begin to break the cycle of self-criticism and allow yourself to grieve in a healthier, more nurturing way. This shift can lead to greater emotional resilience, helping you to navigate the ups and downs of life with more grace and understanding. It's a practice that not only fosters inner peace, but also opens the door to a more compassionate and fulfilling life.

Your Turn

Take a few minutes on this self-compassion exercise (adapted from Johnson & O'Brien, 2013[32]).

Think about an adverse event you've experienced recently or in the last five years. Write down responses to the three instructions that follow in your notebook. Make sure you are honest with yourself as the more effort you put in, the better the results:

1. Write a list of as many ways you can think of in which other people have gone through a similar experience to you.
2. Write a paragraph or two which you express kindness and concern towards yourself, as if you were writing to a friend.
3. Describe your feelings and emotions concerning the event in a non-emotional objective way.

You can review your answers after finishing this chapter.

Let's now look at the components that cultivate self-compassion. According to Professor Kristin Neff, self-compassion entails three components:

1. **Self-Kindness:** This involves being gentle and understanding towards yourself when you face pain or failure, rather than being harshly self-critical. It's about offering yourself the same empathy that you might extend to a friend in a similar situation. In the context of my story, self-kindness played a role when I

experienced the betrayal of the fraudulent agency and the subsequent struggles in Ireland. Rather than being overly critical about what went wrong or blaming myself for the decisions that led me there, self-kindness allowed me to acknowledge the difficulty of the situation, while encouraging a compassionate approach to myself during that time of distress.

2. **Common Humanity:** This aspect emphasises the recognition that suffering and personal shortcomings are part of the shared human experience. When we face challenges, it's easy to feel isolated and believe that our pain is unique. Common humanity helps us realise that everyone goes through tough times, and this realisation can be grounding. For instance, during the ordeal with the agency and the uncertainty I faced in a foreign country, remembering that other students were similarly affected helped me feel less alone. Understanding that setbacks, failures, and even moments of being deceived are part of being human makes the burden of my experiences feel less isolating.
3. **Mindfulness:** Mindfulness is about maintaining a balanced awareness of our emotions, allowing you to observe painful thoughts and feelings without being overwhelmed by them. It helps in neither suppressing nor exaggerating the negative feelings. Mindfulness was helpful, especially during those moments when I felt stuck in Dublin, unsure of what to do next. Instead of letting anxiety or fear take over, acknowledging those emotions and simply letting them 'be' created space for clearer thinking. My decision to focus on the next steps, such as seeking out a new college, despite the hardships, helped me keep away from dwelling too much on what went wrong.

Overall, these three components of self-compassion, self-kindness, common humanity, and mindfulness, could offer a framework for navigating your challenging experiences. By embracing them, you might find strength and resilience in adversity, allowing yourself to move forward with a greater sense of acceptance and inner peace.

Grief is not a linear process, as seen in the illustration on page 88. It's a complex, often messy journey that can feel overwhelming and disorienting. As described in Part 1, the only way we can truly be at peace with the chaotic nature of grief is by letting go of our expectations, by accepting that things are exactly as they are, rather than how we wish them to be. This acceptance is crucial for navigating the emotional turbulence that accompanies loss.

When I was dealing with the grief of losing my mother and friends, I reached a point where I felt completely stuck, as if I were sinking into a deep, dark hole. It was a suffocating experience, one that left me feeling powerless and unable to move forward. This is not uncommon; grief can persist, and for some, it may even evolve into what's known as 'complicated' grief. This type of grief is prolonged and intensified, making it difficult to function in daily life. In such cases, additional interventions may be necessary to help you process your emotions and regain a sense of stability.

Many of us struggle with the fear of asking for help, especially when it comes to something as personal and profound as grief. We may feel that we should be able to handle it on our own, or that seeking help is a sign of weakness. However, this couldn't be further from the truth. Grief is a natural and deeply human experience, but it doesn't mean you have to go through it alone.

There are resources available to help you navigate this unfortunate situation, and seeking support is a sign of strength, not weakness.

Therapists and grief counsellors are trained to guide you through the complex emotions that arise during the grieving process. They can offer coping strategies tailored to your unique experience, helping you to find a path forward even when it feels impossible.

For example, a therapist might work with you to explore and understand your emotions, helping you to process your loss in a healthy way. They may introduce techniques, such as Cognitive Behavioural Therapy (CBT), to challenge unhelpful thoughts and develop more adaptive ways of coping. They can also guide you through mindfulness practices, which can help you stay grounded in the present moment, rather than becoming overwhelmed by feelings of despair.

Letting go of expectations is another crucial aspect of dealing with grief. Often, we have a mental image of how we "should" grieve, or how long the process "should" take. We may expect ourselves to be strong and to move on quickly, but these expectations can add unnecessary pressure and hinder our healing.

It's important to understand that grief doesn't follow a set timeline. Some days you might feel okay, while other days you might feel like you're right back at the beginning. This fluctuation is normal, and by letting go of the expectation that things should be different, you can allow yourself to grieve in your own way and in your own time.

If you find yourself feeling stuck, as I did, it's crucial to recognise that this is a normal part of the grieving process. However, if these feelings persist and begin to interfere with your ability to function, it may be time to seek additional support. Therapists and counsellors can provide the guidance you need to navigate these difficult emotions. They can help you uncover the underlying issues that may be keeping you stuck and work with you to develop a plan for moving forward. In addition to therapy, there are also support groups available, both in-person and online, where you can connect with others who are going through similar experiences. Sharing your story and hearing from others can be incredibly validating, reminding you that you are not alone in your grief.

Grief is a journey that requires patience, self-compassion, and sometimes, the willingness to seek help. By letting go of expectations and embracing the messy, unpredictable nature of grief, you allow yourself the space to heal. And remember, reaching out for support is a courageous step toward healing, not a sign of weakness. You don't have to navigate this journey alone. There are resources, professionals, and communities ready to support you as you work through your grief. Whether it's through therapy, support groups, or simply leaning on a trusted friend, know that help is available, and it's okay to ask for it. In doing so, you honour your own healing process, allowing yourself the time and space needed to emerge from the depths of grief and into a place of peace and acceptance.

In an insightful study by Neff and Germer (2013)[33], the power of self-compassion was put to the test in a pilot study and a randomised controlled trial of the Mindful Self-Compassion (MSC) Program. This eight-week workshop was designed with a simple yet profound goal: to help people become more self-compassionate.

The program wasn't just theoretical; it provided participants with practical, accessible tools they could easily incorporate into their daily lives. For instance, participants were given quick, effective exercises aimed at cultivating a compassionate inner voice and managing difficult emotions. These tools were not only easy to use but also deeply impactful, offering a way to practice self-compassion in real-time, during moments of struggle.

The results were striking. Those who participated in the workshop showed a significant increase in self-compassion, leading to greater life satisfaction. They also experienced fewer symptoms of anxiety and depression compared to those who did not engage in the exercises. This study underscores the transformative power of self-compassion, demonstrating that with the right tools, we can all learn to treat ourselves with the kindness and understanding we deserve, leading to a more fulfilling and emotionally resilient life.

Meditation for Grief and Healing

In the previous chapter, *Keep On Keeping On*, I touched briefly on my early struggles with meditation and some of the myths that often surround the practice. Now, let's dive deeper into truly understanding what meditation is. According to Behan (2020)[34], meditation refers to the formal practice that calms the mind and improves awareness of ourselves, our minds and our environment, whereas mindfulness is being in the present moment.

Meditation is an ancient practice, rooted in traditions that span thousands of years. According to Hari Sharma (2015)[35], there are numerous techniques that help individuals connect to their deeper inner selves. These techniques vary, but they share the common goal of fostering mindfulness and inner peace.

What follows are different types of meditation. It's vital to know that there is no "right" way to meditate, especially in times of grief. Different techniques resonate with different people, and it's worth experimenting to find what works for you during the healing process.

Loving-Kindness Meditation (Metta): This practice involves self-compassion, sending compassionate wishes to yourself and others. During grief, this can be a powerful way to cultivate kindness towards yourself, especially when you might be feeling lost or broken. Start by offering kind phrases to yourself, such as, "May I be gentle with myself," or "May I find peace in this moment." Gradually, you can extend these wishes to the person you've lost, and eventually to others, fostering a sense of connection and love, even in times of pain.

Body Scan Meditation: Grief often manifests physically as tension, tightness, or exhaustion. A body scan meditation guides you through observing the sensations in different parts of your body, helping you release built-up tension. This practice can also bring attention to areas where grief is being held, offering an opportunity for physical as well as emotional release.

Breathing Exercises: Simple breathing exercises, like mindful breathing, are especially helpful during intense emotional moments. Focusing on the breath can provide an anchor when you feel like you're being swept away by waves of sadness. With each exhale, you might imagine releasing a small piece of the pain, allowing the grief to flow more freely.

Guided Meditations for Healing: Listening to guided meditations can be incredibly helpful when it feels too difficult to sit in silence. There are numerous guided practices available that specifically focus on grief and healing. These can provide structure and support when you need it most.

Despite its long history, meditation is often misunderstood. There are many myths and misconceptions that cloud its true purpose. One common belief is that meditation is purely a mental exercise, disconnected from the body, a perception that overlooks the profound mind-body connection inherent in the practice. Another myth suggests that meditation is about stopping your thoughts altogether, which can lead to frustration, especially for beginners. In reality, meditation isn't about silencing the mind, but rather learning to observe and change your relationship with your thoughts.

As we explore the different facets of meditation, we will dispel these myths and uncover the truth about this powerful practice. It's not about achieving a perfect state of mental stillness, but about finding moments of presence and clarity in the midst of life's noise.

Meditation, for many, starts as a tool to manage the overwhelming pace of life. For beginners, the challenge often lies in the frustration of a restless mind, with thoughts running in every direction. The first encounter with meditation can reveal how much we carry with us daily: the stress, the worries, and the constant mental chatter. The practice, however, is not about achieving a complete silence or erasing thoughts, but about changing our relationship with those thoughts. This distinction becomes especially profound when we turn to meditation in times of grief and healing.

Grief – whether from the loss of a loved one, a personal setback, or a deep emotional wound – brings with it an entirely different weight. It's a raw, powerful force that can feel all-engulfing, making it seem impossible to find peace. In moments of deep sadness, meditation may feel counter-intuitive. After all, how can we sit still and do "nothing" when the pain is so intense, when the weight of loss is so heavy on our hearts?

Yet, this is where meditation can offer something truly profound, not an escape from grief, but a space to allow it, to witness it without being consumed by it. The practice provides a safe container for the overwhelming emotions that come with loss, giving us permission to sit with our pain, instead of running from it.

Here are a few ways meditation supports healing through grief:

1. **Creating a space for grief to be felt:** In everyday life, we're often tempted to avoid uncomfortable emotions. But grief needs to be felt in order to heal. Meditation encourages you to sit with your feelings, no matter how painful. You're not asked to push the pain away or force yourself to feel better. Instead, you're invited to be present with what's here, in the moment, whether it's sorrow, anger, or even numbness. This gentle awareness can offer comfort, as you learn to accept your emotions without the need to "fix" them.

2. **Shifting the relationship with pain:** Just as you learned that meditation is about changing your relationship with thoughts, meditation during grief can change your relationship with pain. Instead of seeing pain as something to avoid, meditation helps you meet it with compassion. By observing your grief through a non-judgemental lens, you may begin to see that pain is part of the human experience, something that connects us all. It doesn't mean the pain disappears, but it may feel less overwhelming when you recognise that it's a natural part of love and loss.
3. **Grounding yourself in the present moment:** Grief has a way of pulling us out of the present. We might find ourselves dwelling on memories of the past or worrying about a future without the person we've lost. Meditation gently brings us back to the present moment, grounding us in the here and now. Through practices like mindful breathing, we reconnect with the simple, steady rhythm of life, our breath. Even in moments of intense pain, this focus on the present can be a relief, offering a brief respite from the swirling emotions.
4. **Embracing imperfection in healing:** Healing isn't linear, and meditation reminds us of that. There will be days when sitting in stillness feels impossible, when the emotions are too intense, and that's okay. Some days, meditation may offer comfort and clarity while other days, it might simply be an acknowledgement of your pain. Both experiences are valid.

Through grief, meditation can gradually lead you towards acceptance; not acceptance in the sense of resignation, but rather an acknowledgement of what is. Meditation invites you to accept that grief is part of life, and while the pain of loss is immense, it also reflects the depth of love we hold. This realisation doesn't erase the sadness, but it can soften it, allowing healing to unfold in its own time.

As you continue exploring meditation in this chapter, I encourage you to approach the practice with gentleness. Whether you're dealing with the daily stresses of life or navigating the deep waters of grief, meditation offers a safe space to be with whatever arises. It's not about achieving stillness, but finding moments of peace amidst the chaos, learning to hold yourself with kindness through life's storms, and embracing the healing that comes through presence and patience.

Call to Action

Embrace Meditation as a Path to Healing

Meditation offers a powerful way to navigate the complexities of grief and healing, not by silencing your emotions but by creating a compassionate space to sit with them. I now invite you to take the next step in self-awareness and healing.

1. **Start with Compassion:** Begin your practice by being gentle with yourself. Whether you're grieving or facing a personal challenge, allow yourself to feel what's present without judgement. Take five minutes today to sit quietly, breathe deeply, and simply observe your thoughts and feelings. No need to force 'peace'; just 'be' with what arises. This is a different approach to finding inner calm. Rather than trying to force yourself into a peaceful state, perhaps by ignoring or suppressing difficult thoughts and feelings, this approach encourages simply being present with whatever emotions or thoughts that are arising naturally. This idea is rooted from mindfulness and acceptance. Forcing peace can sometimes create tension as it implies that certain feelings or experiences are not acceptable, which can add stress. Instead, by allowing emotions

and thoughts, experiences to come and go without judgement or resistance, you foster a more genuine sense of ease and presence. It's about accepting the current moment as it is, without the pressure to change it into something "better" or more peaceful.

2. **Choose a Meditation Practice:** Try a form of meditation that resonates with you. Experiment with breathing exercises, body scans, or loving-kindness meditation. Start small, perhaps five to ten minutes each day, and slowly build from there.
3. **Commit to Daily Stillness:** Make a commitment to carve out a few moments each day for stillness. It doesn't need to be long or perfect, but consistency will help you form a deeper connection with yourself and your emotions over time.
4. **Journal Your Journey:** After each meditation session, spend a few minutes journalling. Write down any thoughts, emotions, or insights that surfaced during your practice. This will help you track your healing process and reflect on your progress.
5. **Invite Healing Through Presence:** The next time grief or emotional pain feels overwhelming, instead of pushing it away, invite it into your meditation. See if you can observe it with curiosity and compassion, without trying to change it. You may be surprised by how this simple shift can create a sense of peace and acceptance.

Remember, the path to healing does not go in a straight line, but each moment of stillness brings you closer to finding peace within. Today, take the first step by choosing to be present with yourself. You are stronger than you know, and meditation can guide you through the toughest moments. So, will you take this step towards healing? Start your practice today.

Here is a QR code to a guided meditation video by Jason Stephenson[36], offering you a structured and powerful pathway towards your healing process. Scan the code to access the meditation, allowing it to bring you comfort, emotional expression, and inner peace.

PEARLS OF WISDOM

Deep Grief Is a Reflection of Deep Love

Grief is the price we pay for love. The more we cherish someone, the greater the pain when they are no longer with us.

Though Grief Is Universal, the Journey Is Personal

Everyone experiences grief at some point, but how we navigate it is deeply individual. There is no "right" way to grieve.

Self-Compassion Is Essential in Grief

During times of loss, we often blame ourselves. Learning to treat ourselves with the same kindness and understanding we would offer a friend is key to healing.

Feel the Full Range of Emotions

Grief comes with a whirlwind of emotions, sadness, anger, guilt, and confusion. It's important to give yourself permission to feel these without judgement.

Grief Can Impact Physical Health

The emotional toll of grief can manifest physically, affecting sleep, eating habits, and overall health. Be mindful of the need to care for your body as you process loss.

Faith and Hope Are Powerful Tools for Coping

In the darkest moments of grief, faith in something greater, whether spiritual or personal, can offer a beacon of hope and strength to carry on.

Time Doesn't Erase Grief, but It Transforms It

Grief may never fully disappear, but over time it evolves. We learn to live with the loss, and gradually, the weight of grief becomes more bearable.

It's Okay To Take Breaks and Prioritise Healing

When overwhelmed by grief, it's crucial to give yourself space and time to heal, even if that means stepping away from life's responsibilities for a while.

Connection Helps Ease the Pain

Seeking support from loved ones, friends, or counsellors can provide comfort. You don't have to carry grief alone; sharing it lightens the load.

Honour Your Loss Through Remembrance and Love

Whether through rituals, storytelling, or personal acts of remembrance, honouring the legacy of the ones we've lost can bring solace and keep their memory alive in our hearts.

PART 5

PATIENCE AND PERSEVERANCE

"Patience and perseverance have a magical effect before which difficulties disappear and obstacles vanish."

John Quincy Adams (1767–1848)
6th President of the United States

JOHN QUINCY ADAMS' WORDS capture the essence of two powerful qualities that can transform our approach to challenges: patience and perseverance. When combined, these traits can seem almost magical, making even the most daunting obstacles appear less insurmountable. In this chapter, we'll explore how patience and perseverance work together to bring about success and turn difficulties into stepping stones.

Patience

Patience is often misunderstood as mere waiting or inactivity, but in reality, it is an active, deliberate choice to remain calm and composed in the face of adversity. Dr Sarah Schnitker, an Associate Professor of Psychology and Neuroscience at Baylor

University, defines patience as "the ability to stay calm when facing adversity, waiting, frustration, or suffering."[37] Her research, published in the *Journal of Positive Psychology* in 2012,[38] identifies three main scenarios that test our patience:

1. **Interpersonal Conflict:** Difficulties with colleagues, family dynamics, or managing quirks within relationships.
2. **Life Hardships:** Dealing with chronic illness, systematic racism, or other profound challenges.
3. **Daily Hassles:** The everyday interruptions like traffic jams, flight delays, or being put on hold.

Schnitker's research highlights how impatience can manifest in two ways: explosive reactions, such as screaming or stomping, or complete disengagement, where one gives up entirely. Most of us can relate to these scenarios, as we've all been tested at some point, whether by a traffic jam or a more significant life crisis.

When faced with difficulties, the instinct is often to rush through them, hoping to quickly "fix" the problem. However, rushing usually exacerbates the issue, leading to stress, anxiety, and a lack of clarity. Patience, on the other hand, allows us to step back, understand the situation fully, and approach it with a clear mind. It's a skill that can prevent us from making hasty decisions that we might later regret.

When I was first diagnosed with cancer, my mind immediately raced to the implications for my final year in college. The fear of how this diagnosis would derail my plans was overwhelming. However, rather than rushing to make decisions, I chose to give myself time to process the news. Even after informing my college authorities, who advised me to defer my studies, I decided to stay patient. By allowing myself the space to absorb what was happening, I avoided the stress and regret that might have come from making a hasty decision. This patience granted me inner peace and acceptance of the present moment. I realised the strength I had within me and became open to new possibilities. If

I had rushed to defer, I might still be in school today, regretting that I allowed impatience and fear to dictate my actions.

Patience as a virtue is often undervalued in a fast-paced world that prizes instant gratification. However, research in positive psychology reveals that patience is not only beneficial but crucial for mental well-being, emotional health, and overall life satisfaction. Let's explore each aspect of how patience contributes to well-being and resilience, supported by research in positive psychology.

1. **Stress Reduction**

   Patience is intrinsically linked to stress reduction. When individuals approach situations with patience, they are less likely to experience the acute stress responses triggered by impulsive reactions. Another study by Amanda Al Arja (2023)[39] in *Frontiers in Psychology* found that patient individuals tend to have lower levels of perceived stress. This is because patience enables people to take a step back, assess the situation more clearly, and respond in a way that is thoughtful rather than reactionary.

   - **Mechanisms:** Patience reduces the activation of the body's fight-or-flight response, which is often triggered by stress. By keeping this response in check, individuals can avoid the physiological and psychological toll that chronic stress can impose, such as increased cortisol levels, anxiety, and burnout.

2. **Emotional Regulation**

   Emotional regulation refers to the ability to manage and respond to emotional experiences in a healthy way. Patience plays a pivotal role in this process. According to the aforementioned study by Schnitker (2012; see previous page), patient individuals are better at regulating their emotions, leading to fewer instances of anger, frustration, and anxiety.

- **Mechanisms:** Patience allows for a pause between stimulus and response. This pause is critical for cognitive reappraisal, where individuals can reinterpret or reframe a situation in a way that alters its emotional impact. For example, rather than reacting with anger when faced with a frustrating delay, a patient person might view it as an opportunity to reflect or plan.

3. **Improved Relationships**

   Patience is fundamental in nurturing healthy relationships, be it personal or professional. Relationships thrive on understanding, communication, and empathy, all of which are enhanced by patience. When we are patient, we are more likely to listen fully to others, consider their perspectives, and respond in a way that fosters mutual respect and cooperation.

   - **Research Findings:** Studies in positive psychology indicate that patient people are perceived as more compassionate and empathetic, which strengthens interpersonal bonds. In a study conducted by Schnitker and Emmons (2007)[40], patient individuals reported greater relationship satisfaction due to their ability to navigate conflicts calmly and constructively.
   - **Mechanisms:** Patience prevents the escalation of conflicts by allowing individuals to process their emotions and the emotions of others before responding. This reflective approach leads to more effective communication and resolution of disagreements, ultimately strengthening relationships.

4. **Increased Gratitude**

   Patience enhances our ability to experience and express gratitude. When we are not rushing through life, we become more attuned to the present moment and the positive aspects of our experiences. This mindfulness fosters a deeper appreciation for the small joys and blessings that might otherwise go unnoticed.

- **Research Findings:** A study published in *The Journal of Positive Psychology* by Wood et al. (2010)[41] found that gratitude is closely associated with well-being and life satisfaction. Patient individuals, who are more present and less preoccupied with immediate outcomes, tend to have higher levels of gratitude, which in turn contributes to greater happiness and fulfilment.
- **Mechanisms:** Patience reduces the pressure to constantly achieve or acquire more, shifting the focus from future aspirations to present contentment. This shift in focus allows individuals to cultivate a greater sense of gratitude for what they already have, rather than what they might obtain.

5. **Greater Resilience**

Resilience is the ability to bounce back from adversity, and patience is a key component in building and maintaining resilience. By teaching us to endure challenges without giving up, patience fosters the persistence needed to overcome obstacles and achieve long-term success.

- **Research Findings:** Positive psychology research emphasises the importance of patience in developing resilience. In Schnitker's 2012 study (2012; see previous page), patience was linked to a greater ability to cope with setbacks and a lower likelihood of experiencing depression in the face of difficulties.
- **Mechanisms:** Patience allows individuals to maintain hope and a positive outlook, even when the progress is slow. It encourages a long-term perspective, which is crucial for enduring hardships

and persevering towards goals. Over time, this persistence strengthens resilience, making individuals more capable of handling future challenges.

By reducing stress, enhancing emotional regulation, improving relationships, fostering gratitude, and building resilience, patience can help you navigate life's challenges with grace and strength. In a society that often prioritises speed and immediacy, cultivating patience can lead to a more balanced, fulfilling, and resilient life. Patience is also the foundation upon which perseverance is built. It's what allows us to endure the initial shock of a setback and remain focused on our long-term goals. Once we've cultivated patience, we can then tap into the power of perseverance, the determination to keep moving forward, no matter what.

Patience, combined with perseverance, can lead to extraordinary achievements. Together, they form a powerful duo that can help us overcome even the most formidable challenges, turning what once seemed impossible into a reality. I'll share how I continued to push through obstacles, ultimately realising my goals despite the many challenges that came my way.

Perseverance

In his research on 'Beyond Passion and Perseverance,'[42] Dr Datu defines perseverance as the "relentless determination to continue pursuing a long-term goal despite facing challenges or difficulties". He notes that this steadfastness is closely linked with achieving optimal performance, turning dreams into reality even in the face of adversity.

When I reflect on the obstacles I've faced – losing thousands of dollars to a fraudulent agency, trying to find my footing in a foreign country, and enduring the heart-wrenching loss of my mother and two close friends in quick succession – I often ask myself, "What kept me going? What stopped me from giving up?"

Whenever I share my story, people tell me, "I don't know how you did it. I would have given up." Perhaps you're thinking the same. But ask yourself, would you have given up on your dreams? Would you have let go of everything you've worked for, all because the road became unbearably tough?

Perseverance isn't just about holding on. It's about moving forward, even when the path ahead seems impossible. It's about taking one more step, even when you feel like you can't go on. It's about seeing the goal at the end of the road and deciding that no obstacle is too great to overcome. In the following chapters, I will share how I managed to manoeuvre through these seemingly insurmountable challenges to achieve my goal of settling in a foreign country, returning to college, changing my career, and ultimately becoming an Irish citizen, all while weathering a storm that seemed never-ending.

But before I delve into my own journey, let's explore the stories of a few individuals who exemplify the power of perseverance. These are people who faced monumental setbacks but refused to let those challenges define them. Instead, they chose to push through, becoming beacons of hope and examples of what's possible when you refuse to give up.

Bethany Hamilton: Riding the Wave of Adversity

Bethany Hamilton is an American professional surfer and was thirteen years old when a shark attack left her with one arm. For many, this would have marked the end of their surfing dreams. But not for Bethany. She returned to competitive surfing and defied the odds, becoming an inspiration to countless people around the world. Her story is a testament to the power of perseverance, how a single-minded focus on a passion can turn tragedy into triumph.

Michael Jordan: From Rejection to Greatness

Michael Jordan faced rejection early in his career when he was cut from his high school basketball team. Many would have taken this as a sign to give up. But Michael used it as fuel to work even harder and became one of the greatest basketball players of all time. His perseverance led him to lead the Chicago Bulls to six NBA championships and become a global icon in the process. His story shows that perseverance isn't just about overcoming obstacles; it's about using them as stepping stones to greatness.

Oprah Winfrey: Rising Above the Odds

Oprah Winfrey overcame a difficult childhood marked by poverty, abuse, and numerous challenges, to become one of the most influential women in the world. Despite these hardships, she rose to become a media mogul and philanthropist, changing lives through her work and her words. Oprah's life is a powerful example of how perseverance, combined with self-belief and resilience, can transform even the most daunting circumstances into a platform for success.

Nelson Mandela: The Long Walk to Freedom

Nelson Mandela spent twenty-seven years in prison for his anti-apartheid activism. Many would have been broken by such an experience. But Mandela's perseverance never wavered. Upon his release, he continued to fight for equality and justice, eventually becoming the first Black president of South Africa. His life illustrates that perseverance is often about enduring the unendurable, with the belief that change is possible.

Marie Curie: Breaking Barriers in Science

Pioneering physicist and chemist Marie Curie faced discrimination and countless obstacles as a woman in the male-dominated field of science. Yet she persisted, ultimately winning not one but two Nobel Prizes for her ground-breaking work in radioactivity. Curie's story reminds us that perseverance often requires breaking through barriers and challenging the status quo in the pursuit of knowledge and progress.

Often celebrated as a hallmark of determination and grit, perseverance is far more than simply a personal trait. In the realm of positive psychology, it is recognised as a powerful tool that plays a crucial role in enhancing resilience, fostering well-being, and paving the way for long-term success. Let's delve deeper into how perseverance serves as a cornerstone of positive psychology, supported by research and engaging insights.

1. **Resilience: The Backbone of Perseverance**

   Resilience is the capacity to recover from difficulties, and perseverance is what fortifies this ability. When we encounter setbacks, it is perseverance that keeps us moving forward, transforming failures into learning opportunities rather than insurmountable barriers.

   - **Research Findings:** A study by Angela Duckworth et al. (2007)[43] on grit – a combination of passion and perseverance – demonstrates that individuals with high levels of grit are more likely to achieve long-term goals. Gritty individuals do not view failure as a dead end but as a part of the journey. This mindset is a key component of resilience, allowing them to bounce back from adversity with renewed determination.

   - **Mechanisms:** Perseverance instils a sense of purpose and direction, which is essential for resilience. When we persevere, we develop the mental toughness needed to withstand challenges, and this resilience becomes a self-reinforcing cycle. Each time we overcome an obstacle, our resilience is strengthened, making us better equipped to handle future difficulties.

2. **Optimism: Cultivating a Positive Outlook**

   Perseverance is closely linked to optimism, the belief that positive outcomes are possible even in the face of challenges. When we persevere, we train our minds to see setbacks not as failures but as opportunities for growth and learning.

   - **Research Findings:** Positive psychology research in 1990 by Dr Martin Seligman[44], a leading authority in positive psychology, has shown that optimistic individuals are more likely to persevere in the face of adversity, and this perseverance is linked to better mental and emotional health. Optimism fuels perseverance by providing the hope and belief that efforts will eventually pay off, which in turn fosters a more positive and proactive approach to challenges.

   - **Mechanisms:** Perseverance nurtures optimism by encouraging a growth mindset, the belief that abilities and intelligence can be developed through effort and learning. This mindset shifts the focus from short-term failures to long-term growth, reinforcing the idea that every challenge is a stepping stone to success. As a result, individuals who persevere are more likely to maintain a positive outlook, even when faced with difficulties.

3. **Self-Efficacy: Building Confidence in Our Abilities**

   Self-efficacy – the belief in one's ability to achieve goals – is a critical factor in motivation and success. Perseverance plays a vital role in strengthening self-efficacy by providing repeated experiences of overcoming obstacles and achieving success through sustained effort.

- **Research Findings:** Psychologist Albert Bandura, the originator of Social Cognitive Theory, emphasised that self-efficacy is built through mastery experiences, successes that are achieved after overcoming challenges[45]. Perseverance is central to these experiences. When individuals persevere, they accumulate evidence of their ability to succeed, which boosts their confidence and motivation.

- **Mechanisms:** Perseverance enhances self-efficacy by demonstrating that sustained effort leads to progress. Each time we push through a difficult task, we reinforce our belief in our capabilities. In turn, this growing confidence makes us more likely to take on new challenges, creating a positive feedback loop where perseverance leads to success, and success fuels further perseverance.

4. **Achievement: Turning Dreams into Reality**

   At the heart of every significant achievement lies perseverance. Whether it's mastering a skill, completing a long-term project, or realising a lifelong dream, it is perseverance that drives the consistent effort required to achieve success.

   - **Research Findings:** Longitudinal studies in positive psychology show that perseverance is a strong predictor of academic and professional achievement. For instance, research by Duckworth et al. mentioned on a previous page, found that grit was a better predictor of success than IQ in various contexts, including education and military training. This underscores the idea that perseverance, rather than innate talent, is often the key to achieving long-term goals.

- **Mechanisms:** Perseverance turns abstract goals into actionable plans. By breaking down long-term aspirations into smaller, manageable tasks, perseverance makes the pursuit of these goals more feasible. Each small victory builds momentum, gradually transforming dreams into reality. Furthermore, perseverance fosters a sense of purpose and fulfilment, as individuals see their efforts translate into tangible achievements.

Perseverance is much more than a simple trait; it is a dynamic force that fuels resilience, nurtures optimism, strengthens self-efficacy, and ultimately drives achievement. In the framework of positive psychology, perseverance is a vital tool for enhancing well-being and ensuring long-term success. By embracing perseverance, individuals can navigate life's challenges with determination and grace, turning obstacles into opportunities and dreams into reality. In a world that often values quick wins and instant gratification, perseverance reminds us that true success is born from consistent effort, unwavering resilience, and the belief that we can achieve our goals if we keep moving forward.

In my journey, perseverance was the thread that wove together all the challenges, setbacks, and triumphs. It was the quiet strength that kept me going when everything else seemed to fall apart. And it's what allowed me to not simply survive, but to thrive, achieving my goals even in the darkest of times.

As we continue, I'll share more about how I cultivated this perseverance and how you, too, can harness its power to overcome your own challenges and reach your goals. Because no matter how tough the journey may be, perseverance will carry you through to the other side.

My Story

The summer of 2019 was supposed to be my escape. I had finished my third year of college and was eagerly looking forward to my final year. The long, sunlit days in Ireland were perfect for exploring the countryside, and I made the most of it. The rolling green hills and ancient castles offered a picturesque distraction from the thoughts that lingered at the back of my mind. But no matter how much I tried to lose myself in the beauty around me, something dark and heavy followed me, something I hadn't yet found the courage to face.

A lump on my right breast.

It was a small, almost insignificant thing. But it wasn't supposed to be there. I tried to brush it off, convincing myself it was probably nothing: a hormonal change, maybe, or just my imagination. But my fingers would always find their way back to it, unable to leave it alone. Deep down, I knew this wasn't something I could ignore. But the fear of what it might be was so paralysing that I kept it to myself, not even daring to share it with my family back home in Botswana. The anxiety was a constant, unwelcome companion that shadowed every joyful moment of that summer.

By July, I could no longer pretend it wasn't there. I finally mustered the courage to see my GP, hoping desperately that I was overreacting. But as soon as I saw the look in his eyes, I knew my life was about to change in ways I couldn't even begin to imagine.

My GP was thorough. After a grim examination, he told me that because of my family history of cancer, he was going to refer me urgently to the specialists at the main hospital. I held onto hope that it was all simply a precaution, but the two-week wait for my appointment felt like a lifetime. When the letter finally arrived, summoning me to the Breast Care Clinic, I was shaking so hard that I almost dropped it.

The day of the appointment, I sat in the waiting room, feeling more alone than ever. The walls seemed to close in on me as I silently prayed, begging God for mercy. All I had was my faith and the memory of my late mother to cling to. When the nurse finally called my name, I felt like I was walking to my execution.

The doctor was kind, trying her best to put me at ease. But as she examined the lump, I saw the concern flicker across her face. She excused herself and returned with a senior consultant, who asked me a series of questions that only heightened my fear. When he mentioned an urgent ultrasound and biopsy, the room seemed to spin around me. I felt the cold gel on my skin, but my mind was a thousand miles away, lost in a fog of dread.

The biopsy was over quickly, but the waiting was excruciating. I kept the news from my family, hoping against hope that the results would be clear. But when the call finally came, asking me to return to the hospital for my results, I knew the news wouldn't be good.

Sitting in the hospital lobby, waiting to be called in, I felt like I was on trial for my life. The words of Isaiah 41:10 echoed in my mind, a verse my mother used to recite:

> *"Fear you not; I am with you: be not dismayed; for I am your God: I will strengthen you; yes, I will uphold you with the right hand of My righteousness."*

I clung to those words as I was led into the consultation room.

When the doctor confirmed my worst fears, that I had breast cancer, I felt the ground drop out from under me. I was only 36 years old, alone in a foreign country, and now facing a battle for my life. The doctors recommended immediate surgery to remove the lump and determine the extent of the cancer. I nodded numbly, not absorbing what they were saying. All I could think about was how I wished my mother was alive, how I needed her strength to get through this.

As summer faded into fall, my focus shifted from enjoying my last carefree months before graduation to preparing for surgery. My final year of college was starting, but I had to juggle classes and assignments with endless hospital visits and consultations. It felt like I was living two lives: one as a student, pretending everything was normal, and the other as a patient, grappling with the reality of my diagnosis.

The day of the surgery arrived in mid-August. I was terrified, but I kept telling myself that God wouldn't have brought me this far just to let me fail. The operation went smoothly, and two weeks later, the results came in: ductal carcinoma in situ. The cancer was contained within the milk ducts and hadn't spread to the surrounding tissue. The relief was overwhelming, until the doctor told me that during the surgery, they had found the cancer was starting to break through to other parts of the breast. Another surgery was scheduled to ensure all the cancerous cells were removed.

I decided to keep the news from my family for as long as I could. I didn't want to worry them, especially since they were so far away. But the burden of carrying this secret was crushing. Some days, I would break down completely, overwhelmed by the fear and loneliness. During these moments, I found comfort in the words of Helen Steiner Rice: "There is always hope of tomorrow to brighten the clouds of today. There is always a corner for turning no matter how weary the way…."[46]

Hospitals can feel cold and isolating, and that sense of sterility only deepened the intensity of my experience. Still, I was determined not to let despair consume me.

In January 2020, I faced my fourth surgery, a major procedure involving a mastectomy followed immediately by reconstruction. This wasn't just any reconstruction; I was set to undergo a complex surgery known as the DIEP (deep inferior epigastric perforators) flap. As The Royal Melbourne Hospital explains, the DIEP flap involves carefully transferring skin, fat, and blood vessels from the lower abdomen to rebuild the breast, a highly specialised technique requiring great expertise.[47]

The prospect of an eight to ten hour procedure was daunting, yet I felt profoundly grateful to have access to such advanced care. There I was, thankful for the innovation, the skill of the medical team, and the hope it provided, a powerful reminder that, even in the darkest times, sometimes we find ourselves exactly where we need to be. Since I was kept in the hospital for a couple of days, I had brought with me a copy of *The Alchemist* by Paulo Coelho[48], a book that had always inspired me. The story of Santiago, the young shepherd on a quest for his personal legend, resonated with me deeply. Santiago's journey was filled with obstacles, yet he never gave up. His perseverance reminded me that I had my own journey to complete: finishing my degree and earning my Irish citizenship. These were my personal treasures, and I would have to cross my own desert to reach them.

Throughout this ordeal, I learned the true meaning of patience and perseverance. They weren't simply abstract concepts; they were essential survival tools. Patience allowed me to endure the endless waiting, the uncertainty, and the fear. Perseverance kept me going, even when I wanted to give up.

But how does one cultivate these qualities in the face of such adversity?

Top Tips

1. **Stay Focused On the Bigger Picture:** It's easy to get lost in the pain and fear of the present moment. But keeping an eye on the long-term goals, the things that truly matter, helps to maintain perspective. For me, that was graduating and starting a new chapter of my life.

2. **Cultivate Resilience:** Life throws obstacles at us, often when we least expect them. Facing these challenges head-on and developing coping strategies strengthens both patience and perseverance. I learned that I could handle far more than I ever thought possible.
3. **Maintain a Growth Mindset:** Believing in your ability to grow and improve, even in the darkest of times, fosters patience in learning and perseverance in pursuing your goals. I had to trust that I was strong enough to overcome this, just as Santiago trusted in his journey.
4. **Practice Gratitude:** Reflecting on what you're grateful for can enhance your overall well-being, making it easier to remain patient and persistent. Despite everything, I was grateful for the support of friends, the kindness of strangers, and the strength I found within myself.
5. **Balance Work and Rest:** Overworking yourself can lead to burnout, while proper rest can rejuvenate your energy. I had to learn to pace myself, to listen to my body and mind, and to give myself the grace to rest when needed.

As I navigated this challenging period, I realised that patience and perseverance were more than just survival tactics – they were the keys to unlocking my future. My journey wasn't only about fighting cancer; it was about becoming the person I was meant to be. And in that, I found the strength I never knew I had.

Endurance

Endurance is the ability to sustain both patience and perseverance, especially when the road ahead is long and treacherous. It's about holding onto hope and moving forward, even when the journey seems impossible. There will be moments when every fibre of your being wants to quit, when the weight of your struggles feels unbearable, and when hope seems like a distant flicker. But endurance is not about perfection or endless strength; it's about continuing, even when you're running on empty.

Endurance was what kept me going after my cancer diagnosis, when fear and uncertainty threatened to derail my future. It wasn't about finding the strength to leap over every obstacle at once; it was about patiently navigating each hurdle, one step at a time. There were countless moments when I questioned whether I had the energy to keep moving forward, whether I should give in to the temptation to pause my studies, defer my dreams, and take the "safe" route. But the decision to stay patient, to give myself time to process, to embrace the present moment, was an act of endurance.

In hindsight, I see that this endurance wasn't just about pushing through pain. It was about accepting the reality of my situation, and slowly, day by day, making choices that aligned with my long-term goals. There were no quick fixes, no immediate resolutions. Endurance demanded that I sit with discomfort, uncertainty, and fear, but also to trust that the path I was on would eventually lead to a place of healing and growth.

Endurance is not about being strong all the time; it is about staying in the fight, even when every part of you wants to quit. It's what helped me recover from losing thousands of dollars to fraud in a foreign country, where I felt defeated and alone. That moment could have easily been the end of my journey. I could have packed up and left, surrendered to the belief that I had failed. But I didn't. I kept going. Why? Because deep down, I knew that giving up would only lead to regret. Endurance, in that moment, wasn't a glamorous display of resilience; it was simply putting one foot in front of the other, refusing to be defined by that setback.

And when I lost my mother and two close friends within a short period of time, grief threatened to consume me. Endurance became the anchor that kept me grounded. It didn't take away the pain, but it gave me the strength to carry it with me, to continue living, even when joy felt distant. Grief has a way of making everything feel insurmountable, but endurance teaches us that even in our darkest moments, there's a way through. We don't have to rush the process of healing, but we can commit to the journey.

Your Turn

Think about your own life. When have you faced a situation that felt impossible to overcome? Maybe you're in that place right now, feeling like you've reached your limit? Life has a way of throwing obstacles at us when we least expect it, and it's easy to believe that we can't possibly make it through. You may have heard others say, "I don't know how you got through it. I would have given up." But you didn't give up – you found some spark within yourself, a spark of hope, of purpose, that kept you moving forward, even if it was just one small step at a time.

Endurance is about deciding that no challenge, no obstacle, no setback is too great to overcome. It's about recognising that though the road may be tough, your dreams, your goals, and your purpose are worth the struggle. In moments of hardship, it's easy to lose sight of why we're enduring at all. But remember, your endurance is not only about surviving difficult times; it's about evolving through them. Each trial you face is shaping you, refining your strength, and building the resilience you'll need to face future challenges.

And here's the beauty of endurance: it's cumulative. Every time you push through a difficult moment, you're not just getting through that one challenge – you're building the internal muscles that will help you handle future difficulties. Each time you choose to move forward, no matter how small the step, you're fortifying yourself for the road ahead. You are training your mind, body, and spirit to keep going, even when the way forward is unclear. It isn't about pushing yourself to the point of exhaustion; it's about pacing yourself. When you run a marathon, you don't sprint the entire way. You measure your energy, you take breaks when needed, and you keep your eyes on the horizon, knowing that the finish line is out there, even if you can't yet see it.

So, if you're standing at the crossroads of despair and hope, ask yourself: *Will I let the difficulty of the moment dictate my future? Or will I dig deep, draw on my inner strength, and endure?* The path may be hard, but with endurance, you will come out stronger on the other side. And when you do, you'll look back and realise that every moment of doubt, every challenge you faced, was preparing you for this greater version of yourself.

Endurance is about thriving through adversity, turning pain into purpose, and using every obstacle as a stepping stone towards your growth. Whether you realise it or not, endurance is a quiet, powerful force inside you;one that, when nurtured, will help you conquer even the most daunting of life's challenges.

So, trust in your journey, embrace the process, and remember that every step you take, no matter how small, is a testament to your strength and resilience.

Call to Action

Life often presents us with challenges that we never anticipated, such as a health diagnosis, a personal setback, divorce or even the loss of a loved one. In those moments, patience and perseverance become our greatest allies.

If you are facing your own battle right now, remember that you have the strength to endure, even if it doesn't feel that way. Starting from now, I invite you to challenge yourself and embrace the journey. Embrace the moment by taking things one step at a time, allowing yourself the grace to move forward at your own pace.

Think about a time in your life when you persevered through a challenging time, no matter how small. Ask yourself the following questions and jot your answers in your notebook.

- What was I going through?
- What helped me endure?
- How can I apply that same strength to my current situation?

If you feel overwhelmed, reach out for support, whether from loved ones, a community, or a healthcare professional. Remember, you don't have to walk this path alone.

This exercise helped me immensely during the hardship of my cancer diagnosis. I tried to draw on the strength I had used when my mother's health was deteriorating. I reflected on the perseverance that had carried me through those difficult days.

As I sat there, attempting to journal my feelings, the sadness overwhelmed me. I tried to find the words, but the flood of emotions poured out instead, and I noticed that instead of the marks of a pen on my journal, it was only teardrops.

Recognising I couldn't bear this alone, I made the decision to reach out to the cancer support group. It was one of the best decisions I could have made. The group offered a safe space where I could share my fears, my grief, and my hopes with people who understood exactly what I was going through. They listened without judgement, offered advice, and reminded me that it was okay to lean on others for strength. Through their support, I found the courage to keep going, knowing I didn't have to carry this burden alone. The group became a vital source of strength, hope, and connection when I needed it most.

Commit to treating yourself with kindness and compassion during this journey. Let patience be your anchor and perseverance your guide, knowing that each small victory is a testament to your inner resilience. Start your journey today knowing that, like so many others who have faced difficult battles, you too can persevere and thrive.

PEARLS OF WISDOM

Patience Is Active, Not Passive

Patience is more than simply waiting; it's an active choice to stay calm and composed in the face of adversity. It allows you to fully understand situations and approach them with clarity.

Rushing Often Leads To Regret

When faced with challenges, the instinct to rush can exacerbate problems. Taking the time to process and respond thoughtfully prevents hasty decisions that could lead to regret.

Patience Reduces Stress and Promotes Clarity

By being patient, you can reduce stress and anxiety, allowing for better decision-making and a clearer perspective on the situation.

Perseverance Is Moving Forward Despite Obstacles

Perseverance isn't just about holding on; it's about continuing to move forward, even when the path seems impossible.

Focus On Long-Term Goals

Keeping sight of your long-term goals can help maintain perspective during tough times, ensuring that short-term struggles don't derail your ultimate purpose.

Resilience Is Built Through Adversity

Facing challenges head-on and developing coping strategies strengthens both patience and perseverance, revealing the capacity to handle more than you thought possible.

Adopt a Growth Mindset

Believing in your ability to grow and improve, even in the darkest times, fosters patience and perseverance in pursuing your goals.

Practice Gratitude

Reflecting on what you're grateful for enhances overall well-being, making it easier to remain patient and persistent in the face of challenges.

Balance Work and Rest

Proper rest is essential for maintaining the energy needed to persevere. Overworking can lead to burnout, so it's important to balance effort with rejuvenation.

Adversity Shapes Your True Self

Patience and perseverance aren't just survival tactics; they are essential tools for becoming the person you're meant to be. Challenges often reveal strengths you didn't know you had.

These insights serve as powerful reminders of how patience and perseverance can transform challenges into opportunities for growth and success.

PART 6

SELF-BELIEF

"Believe you can and you're halfway there."

Theodore Roosevelt (1858–1919)
26th President of the United States

COLLINS DICTIONARY DEFINES self-belief as *"confidence in your own abilities and confidence in yourself."*[49]

In this chapter, we'll delve into the essence of self-belief, its profound significance, and practical strategies to develop and maintain it, especially during challenging times.

Understanding self-belief is crucial because it serves as the foundation upon which our actions, decisions, and successes are built. Albert Bandura offers an insightful perspective through his concept of self-efficacy. Bandura defines self-belief as a person's confidence in their ability to complete a task or achieve their goals. According to his Self-Efficacy Theory[45], this belief directly influences our behaviour, the goals we set for ourselves, and ultimately, our success. He likens self-belief to an internal engine that powers our responses to challenges, and shapes our interactions with them.

During times of change or adversity, self-belief can waver or even disappear entirely, leaving us anxious, hesitant, and vulnerable to self-doubt. When this happens, our inner critic often becomes louder, casting doubt on our abilities and pushing us toward inaction.

The Power of Self-Belief

Self-belief is more than a fleeting feeling; it's a powerful force that shapes the trajectory of your life. It influences how you perceive challenges, your resilience in the face of adversity, and your ability to achieve your goals. The stronger your self-belief, the more likely you are to navigate life with purpose and determination.

In the realm of positive psychology, self-belief is closely intertwined with overall well-being and success. Let's explore how this vital attribute impacts various aspects of your life.

Self-Belief Enhances Motivation and Drive

When you have unwavering self-belief, you're more inclined to set ambitious goals and pursue them with relentless determination. This intrinsic motivation is the fuel that powers your efforts, keeping you on track even when the journey becomes arduous. When obstacles arise, self-belief reminds you of your capabilities, pushing you to persevere when others might give up. This inner drive is not only essential for achieving your goals, but also for maintaining momentum and focus in the long run.

Self-Belief Boosts Resilience

Life is full of setbacks, but self-belief equips you with the resilience needed to bounce back. When you trust in your abilities, you're more likely to see challenges as opportunities for growth rather than insurmountable obstacles. This shift in perspective allows you to approach difficulties with a problem-solving mindset, viewing each setback as a stepping stone on your path to success. In essence, self-belief turns failures into valuable lessons, strengthening your resolve to continue moving forward.

Self-Belief Improves Decision-Making

Confidence in your abilities enhances your decision-making process. When you believe in yourself, you're more likely to make decisions with clarity and conviction, without second-guessing your choices. This decisiveness is crucial, especially when faced with tough or time-sensitive situations. Self-belief allows you to trust your instincts, reducing the paralysing effects of doubt and uncertainty. As a result, you're better equipped to take action and make choices that align with your goals and values.

Self-Belief Strengthens Emotional Well-Being

Self-belief plays a significant role in your emotional well-being. A strong sense of self-belief is associated with lower levels of anxiety and depression. When you believe in your ability to overcome difficulties, you're less likely to be overwhelmed by them. This belief acts as a buffer against negative emotions, helping you maintain a positive outlook even during challenging times. In this way, self-belief not only supports your mental health, but also contributes to your overall happiness and life satisfaction.

Self-Belief Fosters Personal Growth

Personal growth often requires stepping out of your comfort zone and embracing new experiences. Self-belief encourages this process by giving you the confidence to take on challenges that may seem daunting. When you trust in your ability to succeed, you're more willing to push your boundaries and explore new opportunities. This willingness to grow and learn is essential for achieving your full potential, both personally and professionally.

Cultivating Self-Belief

While self-belief is a powerful asset, it's not something that everyone naturally possesses. Fortunately, self-belief can be cultivated and strengthened over time, especially during difficult periods. Here are some strategies to help you build and maintain this essential quality.

Reflect on Past Successes

Take a moment to reflect on past challenges that you've successfully overcome. Think about the determination and resilience you exhibited during those times. Remind yourself that you have the strength and ability to succeed, even in the face of adversity. By acknowledging your past achievements, you reinforce your belief in your capabilities and build a foundation of confidence for future challenges.

Set Achievable Goals

Break down your larger goals into smaller, manageable tasks. Each small victory reinforces your belief in your abilities and builds momentum towards achieving your larger objectives. By setting achievable goals, you create a series of positive experiences that boost your confidence and motivate you to keep pushing forward.

Challenge Negative Thoughts

Self-doubt is a natural part of life, but it doesn't have to control you. When negative thoughts creep in, consciously challenge them. Ask yourself whether these thoughts are based on facts or merely fears. Replace them with positive affirmations that reinforce your self-belief. By actively combating negative self-talk, you can shift your mindset from doubt to confidence.

Surround Yourself With Supportive People

Build a network of people who believe in you and your abilities. Their encouragement and support can bolster your self-confidence during challenging times. Surrounding yourself with positive influences can help you stay focused on your goals and remind you of your strengths when you need it most.

Practice Self-Compassion

Be kind to yourself when you face setbacks. Recognise that failure is a natural part of growth and doesn't define your worth or abilities. Practicing self-compassion allows you to treat yourself with the same kindness and understanding that you would offer to a friend. This approach not only helps you bounce back from failure, but also reinforces your belief in your ability to succeed in the future.

Visualise Success

Spend time visualising yourself achieving your goals. Imagine the steps you'll take, the obstacles you'll overcome, and the feelings of accomplishment you'll experience. This mental rehearsal can boost your confidence and prepare you to take on challenges with greater self-assurance. Visualisation is a powerful tool that helps you mentally prepare for success and strengthens your belief in your abilities.

Self-belief is a dynamic quality that grows and evolves as we encounter and overcome life's challenges. It's not only about having confidence in our abilities, but also about nurturing that confidence through experiences that test our resolve. I'd like to share with you my own journey of self-belief, a journey that saw me navigate a cancer diagnosis, embrace leadership opportunities, and achieve goals I once thought impossible. Through this story, I hope to illustrate how self-belief can empower us to face even the toughest challenges with resilience and determination.

My Story

In early 2019, I made a pivotal decision that would shape the course of my life. I joined a non-governmental organisation (NGO) – Junior Chamber International (JCI), Dublin, dedicated to empowering young professionals and entrepreneurs through leadership development. The mission resonated with me deeply, and I was eager to contribute my energy and passion.

However, in July of that same year, my life took an unexpected turn when, as already mentioned, I was diagnosed with cancer. Despite the devastating news, I refused to let it distract me from my commitment to the NGO. I showed up fully, embracing every opportunity to make a difference. Then, in October, as I was en route to receive the results of my second surgery, I received a call from the national president of the organisation. She spoke of an "opportunity," but I was too anxious about my medical results to fully process what she was offering. I asked her to call me back, my mind torn between the anxiety of my medical condition and the curiosity about this new opportunity.

That phone call, however, became a turning point. It diverted my attention away from my fears and towards something positive, an opportunity to focus on instead of my looming diagnosis. After receiving the disheartening news from the doctors about needing a third surgery, I left the hospital and returned the call to the national president. She offered me the role of Master of Ceremonies for an upcoming national event. Without hesitation, I accepted, not fully grasping the magnitude of the event but feeling a renewed sense of purpose.

A few days later, I was informed that my third surgery was scheduled for the Wednesday following the weekend of the event. As I stood there co-hosting, no one could have guessed the battle I was fighting beneath my confident exterior. Behind the scenes, I was managing the fear and physical discomfort of a wound from the previous surgery that required constant care, all while anticipating the upcoming surgery. Yet, in those moments, I felt powerful, focused, and driven by a deep belief that I could handle whatever came my way.

As if that weren't enough, I was also nominated to run for the position of Executive Vice President for our branch, with elections set for Thursday, the day after my surgery. The timing was surreal! Here I was, facing a medical procedure while also contemplating a three-year leadership commitment.

I vividly remember a senior member of the organisation approaching me during the event, concerned about whether I should go ahead with my candidacy given my health challenges. She asked if I was sure I could handle the demands of the role.

My response was resolute: "As long as I can walk and talk, I'm definitely sure I can."

Despite the uncertainty of my upcoming surgery, I maintained a positive outlook, confident that everything would be fine. I even asked if I could record my campaign speech since I wouldn't be able to attend the elections in person.

That Monday, after a weekend filled with highs and the looming reality of surgery, a voice inside me urged me to give up the idea of running for Executive Vice President. But I had already learned the importance of silencing negative thoughts, so I ignored the doubts, picked up my phone, and recorded my pitch.

To my immense joy, I was elected Executive Vice President. The elation of winning that role, coupled with the news, helped me endure the physical pain following surgery. Within just six days, I experienced two major milestones: successfully co-hosting a national event, and being elected to a significant leadership position, all while navigating the challenges of a cancer diagnosis and multiple surgeries.

These experiences taught me the true power of self-belief. I accomplished public speaking at a national and international level, something I had never done before, and I took on a leadership role that would eventually lead me to become President during a pandemic, all while on the road to recovery.

This journey exemplifies what is often referred to as a "self-fulfilling prophecy." When you genuinely believe in your capabilities, your actions align with that belief, leading you to achieve what you set out to do. Self-belief has a profound impact on performance and success. It's a mindset that not only predicts but also creates the outcomes you desire.

Your Turn

Take a moment to pause and ask yourself:

Do I truly believe in myself?

____
____
____

How does my lack of self-belief affect my life?

____
____
____
____
____
____
____
____
____
____
____

How did I feel the last time I believed in myself and successfully overcame a challenge?

____

Note these questions and your answers down in your journal. Doing this exercise will help you gain clarity about your inner strengths and the impact that self-belief (or its absence) has on your daily life. Reflecting on these questions can remind you of past victories and the resilience you've already shown in overcoming challenges. When you connect with that feeling of self-confidence and accomplishment, it can reignite your inner strength and motivate you to face current obstacles with renewed determination. Recognising the role of self-belief in your journey will empower you to embrace your potential, take bolder steps forward, and ultimately thrive in the face of adversity.

Self-Belief and Effective Communication

Self-belief is the foundation of authentic and effective communication, which plays a pivotal role in any relationship, be it personal, professional, or within a leadership context. When you believe in yourself, your communication becomes clear, assertive, and more impactful. This confidence allows you to express your ideas openly, articulate your vision with conviction, and foster deeper connections with others.

During my tenure as Vice President of JCI Dublin, communicating with a diverse group of young professionals required not only skill, but a deep sense of self-assurance. I had to present my thoughts with clarity and conviction, especially when doubts regarding my health or the responsibilities of my role could have easily shaken my confidence. However, my self-belief was the anchor that allowed me to communicate effectively and lead with purpose.

In relationships, whether they are personal or professional, people are drawn to those who speak with confidence and authenticity. When you believe in yourself, it becomes easier to engage in difficult conversations, express your needs, and listen actively to others without feeling insecure. Self-belief in communication fosters an environment of mutual trust and respect, where openness and understanding can thrive.

Top Tips for Building Self-Belief in Communication:

1. **Practice Self-Affirmation:** Before engaging in important conversations, remind yourself of your strengths. Focus on the value you bring to the table.
2. **Prepare and Be Informed:** Confidence often stems from knowledge. Equip yourself with the information and clarity you need to communicate effectively.
3. **Embrace Vulnerability:** Authenticity is key to trust. Don't be afraid to admit when you don't know something or need help. Self-belief isn't about knowing everything; it's about being true to yourself.
4. **Body Language Matters:** Project confidence through your posture, eye contact, and tone of voice. How you present yourself physically can reinforce how you feel internally.

5. **Seek Feedback:** Constructive feedback helps you grow. Seek it from trusted individuals and use it to enhance your communication skills without taking it personally.

When you believe in your own voice, others will believe in it too. Effective communication rooted in self-belief enhances relationships, improves teamwork, and fosters mutual respect. The more confident you are in your own voice, the more you inspire others to believe in themselves, making every conversation a chance to strengthen the bonds between you and those around you.

Self-Belief in Leadership and Empowering Others

Leadership, especially in times of crisis or uncertainty, is deeply influenced by self-belief. The way you perceive your own abilities shapes your decision-making process, your ability to guide others, and your capacity to inspire confidence in those you lead.

When I stepped into the role of President of JCI Dublin during the height of the COVID-19 pandemic, I faced unprecedented challenges. It was a time when every decision had far-reaching consequences, and many situations were beyond my control. Yet, my belief in my leadership abilities and my vision for the organisation allowed me to navigate those uncertainties with confidence. I led with resilience, inspiring my team to trust in our collective ability to overcome obstacles. This sense of self-assuredness wasn't solely about maintaining my own leadership; it was about creating a culture of trust and empowerment that resonated throughout the organisation.

A leader's self-belief has a ripple effect. When you believe in yourself, it encourages others to believe in your vision, trust your decisions, and feel empowered to contribute to the shared mission. Beyond that, as a leader, one of the most impactful roles you can play is to instil self-belief in others. Empowering others is not just about giving them tasks to accomplish but helping them see their potential and the value they bring to the table.

One of my most fulfilling moments as President was encouraging a member who struggled with self-doubt to take on a leadership role. Drawing from my own journey, I reassured her that she was capable and helped her push past her fears. Watching her grow in confidence and eventually excel in her position was a powerful reminder that self-belief doesn't only benefit the individual; it uplifts entire communities.

Top Tips for Building Self-Belief in Leadership:

1. **Lead by Example:** Demonstrate self-belief in your actions. Your team will follow your lead, so when you show confidence in tough decisions, it inspires others to trust your vision.
2. **Acknowledge Setbacks and Learn From Them:** Self-belief doesn't mean ignoring failures. Instead, it is about learning from setbacks and using them to refine your approach without losing confidence in your abilities.
3. **Empower Others:** Offer opportunities for growth and responsibility. By trusting others with leadership roles or tasks, you reinforce their belief in themselves.
4. **Stay Committed to Your Vision:** A strong sense of purpose fuels self-belief. Know your "why" and stay committed to it, even when faced with obstacles. Your persistence will inspire those around you.
5. **Celebrate Wins, Big and Small:** Recognise the achievements of your team and yourself. Celebrating success builds confidence and reminds you that progress, no matter how incremental, is worth acknowledging.

In leadership, self-belief is contagious. The confidence you exude inspires trust, loyalty, and high performance in those you lead. More importantly, when you empower others to believe in themselves, you create a legacy of growth and success that extends beyond your immediate circle. By nurturing self-belief in others, you not only help them realise their own potential, but also create a legacy of empowerment and strength. In leadership, your confidence can be the spark that ignites greatness in those around you.

Call to Action

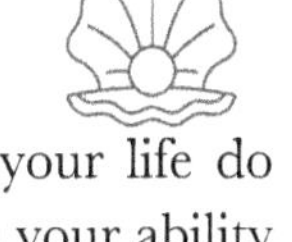

Answer the following questions. Where in your life do you need to cultivate more self-belief? Is it in your ability to communicate openly and assertively with others? Or perhaps in your leadership, where you need to trust your instincts more and empower those around you?

Take a moment to look into these areas where self-doubt is holding you back. Then, commit to small, deliberate actions that will strengthen your self-belief.

- **Set yourself a challenge:** Whether it's having a difficult conversation you've been avoiding, or taking on a leadership role that feels intimidating, push yourself outside your comfort zone.
- **Celebrate your successes:** Keep track of the times when self-belief led you to a positive outcome. Reflect on those moments when doubt creeps back in.
- **Seek support:** Don't be afraid to ask for feedback from mentors, peers, or friends. Sometimes, it takes others to remind us of our own capabilities.

Self-belief is your foundation for a fulfilling, resilient, and impactful life. It's the key to unlocking your true potential, no matter the obstacles you face. Start by nurturing that belief in yourself, and watch how it transforms not only your life, but the lives of those around you.

> You've got everything you need inside of you; now it's time to trust in that and take the next step forward. Believe in yourself, and you'll find that others will, too

Resilience

Resilience is often described as the ability to recover from setbacks and to adapt positively in the face of adversity. In positive psychology, resilience is considered a critical component of well-being and personal growth. The connection between resilience and self-belief is profound, as self-belief serves as the foundation that enables resilience to flourish.

Self-belief, or confidence in one's abilities, is the cornerstone of resilience. Research in positive psychology has consistently shown that individuals who possess strong self-belief are more likely to exhibit resilience in the face of challenges. This is because self-belief empowers individuals to view setbacks not as insurmountable obstacles, but as temporary challenges that can be overcome.

Positive psychology – a field of study that focuses on the strengths and virtues that enable individuals to thrive – offers valuable insights into how self-belief and resilience can be cultivated. One of the key findings in this field is that resilience is not a fixed trait but a dynamic process that can be developed over time. Research has shown that individuals who practice positive thinking, mindfulness, and self-compassion (which I will delve into later on) are more likely to develop resilience. These practices help reinforce self-belief by fostering a positive self-concept and reducing the impact of negative self-talk.

For example, Creswell et al. (2013) in a study titled 'Self-Affirmation Improves Problem-Solving under Stress,'[50] revealed that individuals who engaged in positive self-affirmations were more resilient in the face of stress and more likely to persevere in challenging situations. Their study was influenced by the notion that increased levels of acute and chronic stress are known to impair problem solving and creativity on a large number of tasks. Based on this, they tested whether an experimental manipulation of self-affirmation improved problem-solving performance in chronically stressed participants.

Resilience, in my case, was crucial. Despite the physical and emotional toll of my cancer diagnosis and multiple surgeries, my belief in myself allowed me to keep moving forward. This belief wasn't just a passive feeling but an active force that shaped my responses to adversity. Positive psychology suggests that this kind of resilience is not about avoiding difficulties but about facing them head-on with a belief in one's ability to navigate through them.

In essence, resilience and self-belief are inextricably linked. By fostering a strong belief in your abilities, you lay the groundwork for resilience, enabling you to bounce back from setbacks and emerge stronger on the other side. As you continue to build and reinforce this belief, you'll find that no challenge is too great, no obstacle too daunting. You'll have the resilience to face whatever comes your way, confident in your ability to not just survive, but thrive.

PEARLS OF WISDOM

Self-Belief is the Foundation of Success:

Confidence in your abilities is crucial for overcoming challenges and achieving your goals. It shapes how you respond to adversity and influences every decision you make.

Influence of Self-Belief on Behaviour:

Albert Bandura's Self-Efficacy Theory highlights that self-belief directly impacts your behaviour, goal-setting, and ultimate success. It's like an internal engine that powers your responses to life's challenges.

Self-Belief Enhances Motivation:

A strong sense of self-belief fuels your intrinsic motivation, pushing you to set ambitious goals and pursue them with determination. It keeps you going, even when the journey becomes tough.

Self-Belief Boosts Resilience:

With self-belief, you can view setbacks as opportunities for growth rather than insurmountable obstacles. It equips you with the resilience needed to bounce back stronger from challenges.

Improved Decision-Making:

Confidence in your abilities leads to clearer, more decisive decision-making. When you believe in yourself, you're less likely to be paralysed by doubt and more likely to take action aligned with your goals.

Strengthened Emotional Well-Being:

A strong sense of self-belief is associated with lower levels of anxiety and depression, contributing to better emotional well-being and overall happiness.

Fosters Personal Growth:

Self-belief encourages you to step out of your comfort zone and embrace new challenges. This is essential for personal and professional growth, helping you realise your full potential.

Cultivating Self-Belief:

- **Reflect on Past Successes:** Acknowledge and celebrate your past achievements to reinforce your belief in your abilities.
- **Set Achievable Goals:** Break down large goals into manageable tasks, building confidence with each small victory.
- **Challenge Negative Thoughts:** Actively combat self-doubt by replacing negative thoughts with positive affirmations.
- **Surround Yourself with Support:** Build a network of supportive people who believe in you and your potential.
- **Practice Self-Compassion:** Treat yourself kindly in the face of setbacks, recognising that failure is part of growth.
- **Visualise Success:** Use mental rehearsal to boost confidence and prepare for challenges.

Self-Belief and Leadership:

Self-belief is critical in leadership, as it directly influences your decision-making and your ability to inspire others. Confidence in your abilities helps you lead with clarity and resilience.

Empowering Others Through Self-Belief:

By fostering self-belief in others, you contribute to a cycle of empowerment that extends beyond your immediate influence. Helping others build their confidence enables them to achieve their potential.

Resilience is Linked to Self-Belief:

Resilience – the ability to recover from setbacks – is deeply connected to self-belief. Believing in your abilities helps you face challenges with a positive mindset, making you more likely to persevere and succeed.

These insights underscore the transformative power of self-belief and its role in driving personal success, resilience, and the empowerment of others.

PART 7

RADIANCE OF POSITIVE SELF-TALK

AS HUMAN BEINGS, WE ALL run a constant dialogue in our heads; sometimes giving ourselves instructions, or at other times it is random observations about our environment or situations we find ourselves in. This inner dialogue has a profound influence on how we see ourselves and the world around us. The power of positive self-talk is something I've learned first-hand through some of the most challenging times in my life.

In earlier chapters of this book, I shared how I began to redirect my thoughts towards positivity through self-talk. Radiance within us is defined by the *Cambridge Dictionary* as *"the happiness, beauty, or good health visible in someone,"*[51] and can be nurtured through gratitude, mindfulness, and reframing negative thoughts. An article on *Medical News Today*, titled 'Positive self-talk: Benefits, examples and tips stresses',[52] says that positive self-talk helps cultivate this inner radiance, making us feel good about ourselves, inspiring optimism, and motivating us to keep moving forward, no matter how tough life gets.

My Story

In *Letting Go*, and throughout much of this book, I focused on the challenges life threw at me. These turbulent times tested me in ways I never imagined, but I found solace in the power of positive self-talk. Instead of succumbing to despair, I chose to find strength in my words. Even on the hardest days, when everything seemed overwhelming, positive self-talk became my anchor, helping me focus on the potential for growth, healing, and renewal within myself.

I vividly remember the day I was told I needed a mastectomy. In that moment, I felt a profound disconnection between my body, mind, and soul. But almost immediately, my inner voice stepped in, urging me to stay calm and strong. "Calm down! You can do this! You are stronger than you think! THIS TOO SHALL PASS!" These words echoed in my mind, grounding me when I felt most vulnerable.

This inner voice took me back to another difficult time, when I was told about my mother's passing while I was alone in a foreign country. Once again, the words "THIS TOO SHALL PASS" provided me with comfort and perspective, reminding me that both joy and suffering are temporary and that even the most challenging situations eventually change or improve. During the pandemic, while others worried about the virus, I was juggling the fear of infection, recovering from surgery, overcoming a cancer diagnosis, and completing my final year of college. Positive self-talk became my lifeline. I remember a moment, which I previously mentioned in the chapter on self-belief, when I was given the role of Master of Ceremonies for the JCI Ireland National Convention Ceremony Awards and Gala Dinner. At the time, I had no idea how significant this event would be, but I kept telling myself, "I can do this!"

On the day of the event, I stepped into the grand, beautifully decorated ballroom, and the reality of the situation hit me; my knees started to shake, and nerves threatened to take over. But I kept whispering to myself, "Pearl, you can do this. You've got this!" Slowly, I felt a wave of comfort and confidence wash over me. Thankfully, the evening went smoothly, and the feedback was overwhelming. Many people couldn't believe that it was my first time speaking in front of such a large audience of distinguished delegates.

In this experience, I truly believe that positive self-talk came to my rescue, and I think it's a practice that could benefit you too. This is supported by research,, such as the study by Shadinger et al. (2019)[53], which explored the impact of positive self-talk on public speaking anxiety. Their study found that students who recited a self-affirming statement just before giving a speech or presentation experienced a greater reduction in anxiety compared to those who didn't. My experience mirrored their findings; I was able to transform my anxiety into a sense of empowerment, and I believe the right mindset can make all the difference.

The habit of positive self-talk grew my inner strength, like a flower pushing through the cracks in concrete. I became less anxious, less prone to imagining the worst. A study conducted by Sadri Damirchi et al. (2020)[54] highlighted a significant positive relationship between self-talk and problem-centred coping strategies during the COVID-19 pandemic. It suggested that self-talk greatly influenced how people coped with anxiety during that difficult time. For me, self-talk was a crucial coping strategy that helped me navigate my healing process in the middle of the pandemic.

Silencing the Inner Critic

We all have an inner critic: a voice inside our heads that often magnifies our doubts, fears, and insecurities. This inner voice can be particularly loud during moments of vulnerability, failure, or uncertainty. It tells us we're not good enough, capable enough, or that we'll never succeed, leading us down a path of self-doubt. In moments of crisis, such as the one I faced during the pandemic while recovering from surgery, the inner critic can become almost deafening. But it's in these very moments that silencing this voice becomes most critical.

I remember receiving a phone call from the hospital informing me that all my medical appointments had been cancelled due to the pandemic. As a cancer patient, still healing from surgery, I was advised to isolate completely. Although I had anticipated this call, hearing the reality of it sent a wave of shock through me. Alone in a foreign country, far from my family, fear and anxiety gripped me, and my inner critic took full control. I now had to be my own nurse, physio, doctor, everything.

I found myself overwhelmed with unanswerable questions that amplified my despair:

- What if I die here alone? Who will find me?
- What if my wounds get infected and I can't go to the hospital?
- What if I never walk straight again?
- Does this mean all the effort, money, and time I've invested in pursuing my dreams have been in vain?
- Will I ever get a chance to go back to work?

Each attempt to answer these questions only heightened my anxiety, feeding the voice that told me I was helpless and alone. In my desperation, I did something I never thought I would, I called my late mother's mobile number, longing for her comfort. I was hesitating but I eventually pressed 'Call'. Seeing the word 'Mum' on the screen brought a rush of emotions. When the call connected, I nearly collapsed from the shock. A young lady answered, and I introduced myself.

"Hello, my name is Letlotlo. I'm very sorry to be calling you, but this is my late mother's mobile number, and I miss her so much during this trying time. I know this may sound strange, but I needed to see 'Calling Mum' on my screen."

To my surprise, though it was an unusual situation, the young lady listened kindly and reassured me. For a few days, I kept calling, but soon realised that these conversations, while comforting, were only temporarily soothing my deeper wounds.

It wasn't until one particular day, crying in the bathroom, that I truly understood the power I had within myself to silence the inner critic. I caught a glimpse of myself in the mirror and, in that reflection, I imagined my mother's voice speaking to me.

"Letlotlo, I'm here with you. You are not alone, and things will get better," I heard her say.

I repeated these words out loud, mimicking her comforting tone. And in that moment, I felt an immense wave of calm and hope wash over me.

This experience taught me a profound lesson, one that can help anyone battling their own inner critic. Silencing that negative voice isn't simply about ignoring it. It's about replacing it with compassionate, supportive self-talk. When I began speaking to myself the way my mother would, with love and reassurance, the inner critic started to lose its power. I discovered that I could be my own source of comfort and strength, even in the darkest moments.

Silencing the inner critic doesn't mean that you'll never experience self-doubt or fear again, but it does mean that you can choose not to let that voice dominate your thoughts. Instead, you can learn to counteract it with kindness, self-compassion, and positive affirmations. It's about turning the volume down on the doubts and insecurities that hold you back and amplifying the inner voice that tells you, *"You are enough, and you will get through this."*

In those moments when you feel overwhelmed by fear or self-doubt, take a moment to pause. Recognise the inner critic for what it is – just a voice, not the truth – and choose to speak to yourself as you would to someone you love. Replace the negativity with words of encouragement, and you'll find that you have the power to quiet the critic, even in your most difficult times.

The Power of Words: Shaping Your Reality

Practicing positive affirmations is like rewiring your mind with short, powerful statements that challenge and overcome self-sabotaging thoughts. By consistently repeating these affirmations and believing in them, you can create positive changes in your life, empowering yourself to build confidence and live a fulfilled, purposeful life. Positive affirmations are present-tense, intentional statements that affirm your abilities, values, and goals. They harness the brain's neuroplasticity, the brain's ability to reorganise itself by forming new neural connections, in order to adopt a more optimistic and constructive way of thinking. When you consistently repeat positive affirmations, you effectively rewire your brain to support a healthier, more positive mindset.

The concept of positive affirmations is beautifully illustrated in the film *The Pursuit of Happyness* (2006)[55], based on the true story of Chris Gardner, portrayed by Will Smith. Despite facing homelessness and extreme hardship, Gardner's unwavering belief in himself and his persistent use of positive affirmations were crucial in his journey from poverty to becoming a successful stockbroker. His mantra, "I can", exemplifies how self-belief and positive affirmations can lead to remarkable achievements, even when the odds are stacked against you.

In my own life, positive affirmations have been a cornerstone of my resilience and growth. I have sticky notes with positive affirmations placed around my home, with my favourite one on the bathroom mirror. This daily reminder sets a positive tone for my day, instilling a sense of purpose and confidence. Even during the most challenging times, such as struggling to walk after surgery, the affirmation "This too shall pass" by my bedside provided comfort and reassurance that pain and hardships are temporary.

If you're someone who struggles with self-doubt or negative self-talk, incorporating positive affirmations into your daily routine can gradually shift your mindset.

Creating a Habit of Positive Self-Talk

By cultivating the habit of positive self-talk, you are gradually training your brain to look for the good, to speak to yourself with kindness, and to challenge the negativity that often creeps in. Building this habit is crucial because the thoughts we repeat to ourselves shape our self-image, affect how we approach challenges, and even influence the outcomes we experience in life. If you've ever found yourself stuck in a spiral of self-criticism or doubt, you know how draining that can be. On the other hand, a habit of positive self-talk can create a foundation of inner strength, resilience, and confidence, allowing you to face adversity with a more empowered mindset.

The process begins with awareness, recognising when your self-talk is working against you and consciously choosing to shift it. Like training a muscle, it requires repetition, patience, and commitment, but over time, positive self-talk can become your default mode of thinking. It becomes less of a forced practice and more of a natural way of relating to yourself, nurturing your inner radiance.

As you begin to consistently practise, you'll notice a shift not only in how you view yourself but also in how you respond to the world around you. Positive self-talk transforms your inner dialogue into a supportive, uplifting force, empowering you to take on challenges with greater courage and optimism. By creating this habit, you're laying the groundwork for long-lasting mental and emotional well-being.

Action Steps

Here is a simple exercise designed to help you integrate positive affirmations into your life through journalling, reflection, and repetition:

Step 1: Identify Your Core Affirmations

Start by identifying three to five positive affirmations that resonate with you and write them in your journal or the space provided. These should reflect your goals, values, and the mindset you want to cultivate. Ensure they are in the present tense, specific, and meaningful to you. Examples include:

- "I am capable and confident in everything I do."
- "I am deserving of love and respect."
- "I embrace challenges as opportunities for growth."
- "I am in control of my thoughts and emotions."
- "I attract success and positivity into my life."

Your Turn

Affirmations…

____

____

____
____
____
____
____
____
____
____
____
____
____
____
____
____
____
____
____

Step 2: Create a Daily Affirmation Journal

In your journal/notebook or a digital journal, write your affirmations each day. Select a time that works best for you. Many find that morning affirmations are most effective, while others prefer doing it before bed.

Daily Routine:

1. **Morning Practice:** Upon waking up, write down your chosen affirmations in your journal. As you write each one, say it aloud to yourself. This reinforces the message both visually and audibly.
2. **Evening Reflection:** At the end of the day, revisit your affirmations. Write them down again and reflect on how they influenced your thoughts and actions throughout the day. Did you notice any shifts in your mindset? Were there moments where these affirmations helped you navigate challenges?

Step 3: Reinforce With Visual Cues

In addition to your journal, place your affirmations in visible spots around your home or workspace. Use sticky notes, posters, or phone reminders to keep these positive statements in front of you. The more you see and repeat them, the more they become a natural part of your thought process.

Step 4: Engage in Positive Self-Talk Throughout the Day

Throughout your day, consciously practice positive self-talk. When you catch yourself thinking negatively or doubting your abilities, pause and replace those thoughts with your affirmations. For example, if you start thinking, "I can't do this," immediately counter it with, "I am capable and confident in everything I do."

Step 5: Review Your Progress Weekly

At the end of each week, review your journal entries and reflect on any changes you've noticed in your self-talk, mood, and overall mindset. Are you feeling more positive? Are you catching negative thoughts more quickly? Celebrate any progress, no matter how small, and continue to refine your affirmations as needed.

PEARLS OF WISDOM

Here are some strategies to help you practice positive self-talk consistently.

1. Avoid Falling into the Negative Self-Talk Trap

The first step in practicing positive self-talk is recognising and avoiding negative thinking. Often, negative thoughts fall into these categories:

- **Personalising:** Blaming yourself for everything. I struggled with this, often blaming myself for my mother's passing, thinking that if I had stayed longer in Botswana, she might still be alive. This kind of thinking only fuelled my anxiety and frustration.
- **Magnifying:** Focusing solely on the negative aspects of an experience, to the point where you overlook any positive outcomes. Psychologists Tedeschi and Calhoun introduced the concept of Post-Traumatic Growth in the mid-nineties, arguing that adverse life events can lead to positive changes. If you magnify the negatives, you might miss out on acknowledging the growth and positive changes that come from challenging experiences.
- **Catastrophising:** Always expecting the worst. After my cancer diagnosis, I often caught myself thinking, "I might die" or "What if I don't wake up from the anaesthesia?" This type of thinking is common but counterproductive.
- **Polarising:** Seeing things in black and white, without recognising any middle ground. Being aware of these patterns can help you identify triggers and shift your mindset.

2. Talk to Yourself Like You Would a Friend

Be gentle, compassionate, and encouraging with yourself. When you catch yourself engaging in negative self-talk, evaluate the root cause and respond with affirmations that highlight your strengths. For instance, stand in front of a mirror and verbally express the things you are thankful for in your life.

A Personal Example: During the pandemic, after surgery and final exams, I was devastated to hear that our graduation would be held online. I told myself, "This is it. I'm not working, I'm not allowed to leave the house, I'm not well. I'm really done." This negative self-talk deepened my despair. However, recalling my mother's comforting words, "Letlotlo, wipe off those tears and focus," I gained the strength to persevere. I wrote a letter to myself filled with praise, encouragement, and love, then read it aloud in the mirror. This act of self-compassion transformed my feelings, proving the power of positive self-talk.

Here is the letter I wrote to myself:

Dear Pearl,

Pearl, you have been through a lot to give up now. You are not useless. Please be grateful for all your achievements.

You have achieved your long-term goal of going back to college, as you promised your mother. Stop being hard on yourself. Yes, it seems blurry now, but be hopeful that everything will fall into place.

You are STRONG, Pearl!

Look at what you have been through. I mean, seriously; please be positive. It is not as bad as it may look; you will definitely pull through this as well. Just hang in there.

I LOVE YOU, PEARL!

Yours,
Pearl

After writing that letter to myself, I felt a profound sense of relief and a renewed perspective on my own worth. The letter didn't simply give me a fleeting moment of comfort, but became a source of strength that I returned to whenever I faced challenges. Even today, when self-doubt or difficult situations arise, I revisit that letter, and it continues to uplift and encourage me.

Call to Action

I encourage you to try this for yourself. Write a letter, either below or in your notebook, to the version of you that needs encouragement, understanding, and support. Pour your heart into it, acknowledging your strengths, your struggles, and your resilience. Then, whenever you need a boost, return to those words. You'll find that the letter becomes a powerful reminder of your inner strength and the progress you've made. It's a simple act of self-compassion that can have a lasting impact on your life, just as it has on mine.

3. Practice Gratitude and Mindfulness

Focus on the good in your life and stay present in the moment. Gratitude and mindfulness can help shift your perspective and reinforce positive thinking, further enhancing the effectiveness of your affirmations.

Positive self-talk is not a one-day journey; it requires consistency and dedication. However, the rewards are invaluable. By regularly engaging in positive self-talk and writing down affirmations, you create a habit of reinforcing positive beliefs about yourself. Over time, this practice leads to a more optimistic outlook, greater self-confidence, and an overall improvement in your mental and emotional well-being.

Remember, the way you speak to yourself shapes your reality. Embrace positive affirmations as a daily practice, and watch as they transform your life, as they did mine.

PART 8

VISUALISATION

Make Your Dreams Your Reality

"Visualisation is daydreaming with a purpose."

Bo Bennett (1972–)
American businessman and author

VISUALISATION IS MORE than just a daydream; it's a powerful tool that bridges the gap between our present selves and our desired futures. By mentally rehearsing your goals, you not only define them more clearly but also prime your mind to achieve them. Both positive self-talk and visualisation have been shown to be effective in enhancing performance and achieving success. *Cambridge Dictionary* defines visualisation as "*the act of forming a picture in your mind of something you want to achieve, in the belief that doing so will make it more likely to happen*".[56]

In this chapter, we'll also explore the profound impact of visualisation on motivation and confidence, and how these concepts can help you achieve your goals.

Visualisation can be likened to viewing life through a special lens that sharpens our focus on our deepest desires. It's a mental exercise where we picture our goals as already accomplished, creating a vivid image of success in our minds. Athletes have long used this technique to enhance their performance. Here is an example…

In 1942, a boy was born in Louisville, Kentucky, a descendant of slaves from the Antebellum South. Growing up, he struggled with dyslexia which made school a challenge, and he faced the harsh realities of racial segregation. One day, he was denied a simple bottle of water at a shop solely because of the colour of his skin.

Despite the odds stacked against him, this boy grew up to become one of the most influential and celebrated athletes of the twentieth century, Muhammad Ali. Ali's belief in the power of visualisation played a crucial role in his journey to greatness. He wasn't born with a silver spoon or a head start; he harnessed the inner strength that we all possess but often overlook.

Ali famously said, "If my mind can conceive it and my heart can believe it, then I can achieve it." His story is a testament to the idea that you don't need to be an expert in personal development to tap into the power of visualisation. All it takes is a clear vision, unwavering belief, and the courage to pursue your dreams. Like Ali, you too can unlock your potential and achieve your goals, no matter the challenges you face.

Jim Carrey, one of today's most successful actors, shared a story about how, when he was still a struggling actor in the early 1990s, he wrote himself a cheque for $10 million for "acting services rendered." He carried this cheque in his wallet as a daily source of inspiration. Years later, Carrey landed a role in the film *Dumb and Dumber*[57] that paid him exactly $10 million.

Similarly, media mogul Oprah Winfrey, one of the wealthiest women in the world, practiced visualisation from a young age. Oprah has often spoken about how she envisioned a better life for herself, different from the hardships she observed her grandmother enduring. She famously said, "Create the highest, grandest vision possible for your life, because you become what you believe."

These examples underscore the power of visualisation. By vividly imagining a desired future, we can motivate ourselves to take the necessary steps to make it a reality.[58]

My Story

Let me share with you how visualisation became a lifeline for me during one of the most challenging periods of my life. In March 2020, during the first COVID-19 lockdown, I was recovering from surgery and dealing with a cancer diagnosis. As a high-risk patient, I was confined to my home, and the isolation, coupled with the fear and uncertainty, often left me feeling hopeless. On one particularly difficult day, a switch flipped in my mind. I began to ask myself, "Pearl, when this is over, how do you want to see yourself? What are your heart's desires? What do you want?"

The questions came fast, but the answers were elusive. This lack of clarity frustrated me further, leading to tears and feelings of despair. But I realised that crying wasn't going to help me. I needed to act, even if it was just within my own mind. That's when I decided to conduct what I called a "self-workshop."

The idea of a self-workshop might sound odd, but it was inspired by childhood memories of my late neighbour Becky, who loved playing schoolteacher with imaginary students. Becky, who was like a sister to me, would line up chairs and conduct lessons for her invisible class. In my loneliness during the lockdown, I decided to adopt Becky's childhood game. I envisioned ten versions of myself attending a workshop, and I was the facilitator.

Self-Workshop: Crafting Your Vision for the Future

The first workshop I held for myself was about creating a vision board, a visual representation of my goals and desires. I focused on several key areas of my life, and here's how I used visualisation to reshape my future.

Health and Wellness

Given my recent surgery and cancer diagnosis, health and wellness were at the top of my agenda. I visualised myself as healthy, strong, and full of energy. I imagined myself exercising at home, eating nutritious meals, and taking care of my mental health. In my mind, I could see a future version of myself who had not only overcome the challenges I was facing but was thriving. A song that resonated deeply with me during this time was Michael Bolton's *When I'm Back on My Feet Again.*[59] The lyrics about resilience became a mantra for me and helped me picture my recovery, giving me the strength to push through each day.

Career and Professional Growth

Even though the pandemic made my professional future uncertain, I refused to give up. I visualised myself graduating from my degree program, securing a new job that was less demanding on my health, and eventually pursuing a master's degree and a PhD. I saw myself walking across the stage in a cap and gown, holding my diploma, and later, accepting a job offer that aligned with my new life goals. These images gave me hope and the motivation to keep moving forward, even when the path ahead seemed unclear.

Lifestyle and Experiences

This was perhaps the most exciting part of my vision board. I dreamed of travelling the world, beginning with France, where I would visit the Eiffel Tower. I also imagined celebrating a white

Christmas in Norway, surrounded by snow-covered landscapes that I had only seen on postcards and TV. Growing up in Botswana, I had always been fascinated by the idea of a snowy Christmas, and now I was determined to make that dream a reality.

Another powerful image I included on my vision board was a book with my picture and name on the cover and a 'bestseller' sticker. This represented my aspiration to become a published bestselling author, a goal that inspired me to start writing the very book you're reading now!

Creating my vision board during such a difficult time brought me joy and a sense of purpose. It allowed me to mentally escape the confines of my apartment and imagine a brighter future. As I carefully selected and arranged the images, I felt a renewed sense of hope and determination.

Visualisation is not only a feel-good exercise; it's backed by science. A study published in *Neuropsychologia*, 'From mental power to muscle power – gaining strength by using the mind,' Ranganathan et al. (2004)[60], explored whether mental training could induce strength gains without physical exercise. The researchers found that simply imagining moving certain parts of the body could almost train the muscles as effectively as actual movement. This study highlights the mind's incredible power to influence the body, and it underscores the potential of visualisation as a tool for personal growth.

Bringing Your Dreams to Life

Once you've identified the core areas for your vision board, the next step is to envision the details. What does your dream job or lifestyle look like? Who are you surrounded by in your most fulfilling relationships? What does a day in your ideal life feel like?

Action Steps

Now that you understand the power of visualisation, let's explore how you can incorporate this practice into your own life. Whether you're aiming to achieve specific goals or simply want to foster a more positive mindset, visualisation can be a transformative tool.

1. Create a Clear Vision

Begin by identifying what you want to achieve. This could be related to your career, health, relationships, or any other area of your life. The key is to be as specific as possible. Instead of vaguely wishing for success, picture what success looks like for you. Where are you? What are you doing? Who is with you? The more detailed your vision, the more powerful your visualisation will be.

2. Use All Your Senses

When visualising, engage as many senses as possible. Imagine not only what your goal looks like, but also what it sounds, feels, smells, and even tastes like. For example, if you're visualising a successful business presentation, picture yourself standing confidently in front of an audience, hear the applause, feel the weight of the microphone in your hand, and sense the satisfaction of a job well done.

3. Make It a Daily Practice

Visualisation should be a regular part of your routine. Set aside a few minutes each day to close your eyes and immerse yourself in your vision. Morning is an ideal time, as it sets a positive tone for the rest of the day.

Alternatively, you can visualise before bed, allowing your subconscious mind to work on your goals while you sleep.

4. Create a Vision Board

A vision board is a physical representation of your goals. It's a collage of images, words, and quotes that inspire you and reflect what you want to achieve. Place your vision board somewhere you'll see it every day, such as your bedroom or office. Each time you look at it, take a moment to connect with your vision and reaffirm your commitment to your goals.

5. Let Your Vision Inspire Action

Visualisation alone isn't enough; you need to take action. Allow your vision to guide your decisions and motivate you to take the necessary steps towards your goals. Each action, no matter how small, brings you closer to making your vision a reality.

6. Speak It Into Existence

Affirmations are a powerful complement to visualisation. By speaking your goals out loud as if they've already been achieved, you reinforce your belief in their attainability. For example, instead of saying, "I want to be healthy," say, "I am healthy, strong, and full of energy."

7. Pray and Meditate on Your Vision

If you're spiritually inclined, consider incorporating prayer into your visualisation practice.

The Bible says:

Therefore I tell you, whatever you ask for in prayer, believe that you have received it, and it will be yours. (Mark 11:24).

By combining visualisation with prayer, you align your desires with your faith, adding another layer of power to your practice.

8. Leave Room for Growth

When creating your vision board or visualising your goals, leave some space for new opportunities and desires to emerge. Life is dynamic, and your goals may evolve over time. By keeping an open mind, you allow for the possibility of even greater things than you initially imagined.

During my self-workshop, I followed these steps to create a vision board that reflected my deepest desires. I carefully selected images and quotes that resonated with my goals and aspirations, and I placed them in areas of my life that I wanted to focus on: health, career, lifestyle, and experiences.

This process was not only enjoyable but also deeply transformative. It gave me a sense of control during a time when so much was uncertain. By visualising my future and creating a tangible representation of my goals, I was able to shift my mindset from one of fear and anxiety, to one of hope and determination.

By creating vivid mental images of our desired outcomes, we engage our imagination and tap into the power of our subconscious mind.

Top Tips

Here are some of the key benefits of visualisation:

1. **Clarifying Goals**

   Visualisation is like turning on a light in a dark room: it illuminates the path forward, helping you see your goals with greater clarity. When you engage in visualisation, you aren't just daydreaming; you're creating a mental map that guides your actions. By picturing your desired outcomes, you start to understand not only what you want, but why you want it. This understanding is crucial because it gives your goals a sense of purpose and direction.

   For example, when I was recovering from surgery during the pandemic, I used visualisation to clarify my goals for health and wellness. I didn't only imagine myself feeling better; I saw myself thriving, exercising regularly, and living a balanced, healthy life. This mental image wasn't vague; it was detailed and specific. I could see myself going for morning walks, preparing nutritious meals, and even listening to uplifting music that energised my spirit. This clarity helped me understand my "why" – I wanted to regain control of my life, feel empowered in my body, and embrace a future full of vitality. With this clear vision, I was able to focus my energy on the steps that would lead me to that reality, such as committing to a daily exercise routine and eating healthier.

2. **Enhancing Motivation**

   Visualisation is a powerful motivator because it bridges the gap between your present self and your future self. When you vividly imagine your desired future, you create a strong emotional connection to that vision. This emotional connection acts like a fuel that keeps your inner fire burning, driving you to act, even when the going gets tough.

During my recovery, I faced many days when it was hard to stay motivated. The isolation, the uncertainty, and the physical challenges were overwhelming at times. However, each time I visualised myself healthy, happy, and achieving my goals, I felt a surge of motivation. I saw myself not just surviving but thriving, graduating, getting a fulfilling job, and experiencing the joys of life, like travelling to Paris. This vivid image of my future self was so compelling that it pulled me forward, even on the hardest days. When I finally got that office job in January 2021, I realised that my visualisation had created a powerful connection between my current efforts and my future success. It wasn't simply about imagining the result; it was about staying motivated through every small step along the way.

3. **Boosting Confidence**

   Confidence is often the difference between success and failure. When you visualise yourself achieving your goals, you build a mental narrative of success. This narrative isn't simply a fantasy; it's a powerful tool that programs your mind for success and strengthens your belief in your abilities.

When I was visualising my goals, I didn't only see the outcome; I saw myself overcoming obstacles and succeeding despite challenges. For example, when I imagined myself walking the streets of Paris or experiencing a white Christmas in Norway, I didn't only see the beautiful scenery. I also saw the journey that got me there: completing my degree, securing a stable job, and planning my travels. Each time I revisited these visualisations, I reinforced the belief that I could achieve these dreams. This repeated imagery helped to boost my confidence. I began to believe that if I could see it in my mind, I could achieve it.

When I finally stood in front of the Eiffel Tower in September 2022 and experienced my first white Christmas in Norway later that year, it wasn't just a dream come true – it was a testament to the power of visualisation. These experiences weren't simply lucky breaks, but were the result of a confident belief in my abilities, fuelled by the mental imagery I had practiced. This confidence allowed me to take risks, like pursuing new job opportunities and planning international travel, that I might have shied away from if I hadn't visualised myself succeeding.

When you practice visualisation, you're not just wishing for success, you're actively preparing your mind and spirit for it. Whether it's clarifying your goals, enhancing your motivation, or boosting your confidence, visualisation is a powerful tool that can transform your dreams into reality. My journey is proof of that.

PEARLS OF WISDOM

Steps to Amplify the Power of Your Vision Board

Now that you've created your vision board, how do you use it to amplify the law of attraction and manifest the future you've mapped out for yourself? Here are some steps you can take:

Let Your Board Inspire Action

Your vision board should be more than simply a collection of images; it should serve as a constant reminder to take small steps toward your goals. Each time you look at your board, let it inspire you to take action, no matter how small.

Speak It Into Existence

A powerful way to manifest your desires is to speak them out loud as if they've already come true. Use affirmations to reinforce your belief in the possibilities that your vision board represents.

Continue Including Your Heart's Desires in Prayer

For those who pray, continue to include your heart's desires in your prayers. As Mark 11:24 suggests, believing that you have already received what you ask for in prayer can bring your desires to fruition.

Leave Some Spaces Open on Your Vision Board

Leaving some space on your vision board allows room for new opportunities and desires to emerge. This openness invites the unexpected into your life, making room for growth and expansion.

Call to Action

Activity: Conduct Your Own Self-Workshop

During your spare time, try conducting a self-workshop like I did. Reflect on your goals, create a vision board, and immerse yourself in the process. It may seem simple, but it can work wonders in helping you achieve clarity, motivation, and confidence.

Visualisation is a powerful tool that can transform your life by helping you clarify your goals, enhance your motivation, and boost your confidence. By creating vivid mental images of your desired future and using tools like vision boards and affirmations, you can align your thoughts and actions with your goals, making them more attainable. Remember, while visualisation is a powerful starting point, it must be coupled with action. Let your vision guide you, inspire you, and propel you forward on your journey to success.

In a *Forbes* article (2014) titled 'Dr Myles Munroe: On Leadership, Vision, Purpose, and Maximizing Your Potential,'[61] the late Dr Myles Munroe (1954–2014), a renowned Bahamian pastor, motivational speaker, and author, shared a powerful perspective on purpose and vision. He emphasised, "Purpose is when you know and understand what you were born to accomplish. Vision is when you see it in your mind and begin to imagine it." Dr Munroe's teachings have left a lasting legacy, inspiring countless individuals to not only identify their life's purpose but also to visualise and work towards achieving their full potential. His words remind us that true leadership starts with a clear understanding of our purpose and the ability to envision the path forward.

By envisioning what you desire, you set a clear trajectory for your life, and with determination and effort, you can bring your dreams to life.

Manifesting With Emotion: The Power of Feeling Your Vision

Visualisation is more than just creating images in your mind; it's about emotionally connecting with your vision. When you not only see your future but also feel the joy, excitement, and fulfilment it brings, you ignite the motivation and belief needed to turn that vision into reality. It's this emotional connection that fuels your commitment and drives you forward, even when challenges arise.

Now that you've identified what you want for your life, it's time to take it a step further by deeply experiencing the feelings associated with your goals. Imagine what it would feel like to have already achieved them. Envision yourself living that reality: how does it feel to wake up in the life you've worked for? Let that sense of accomplishment, gratitude, and joy wash over you.

To help you fully immerse yourself in this emotional experience, here is a guided visualisation video. It will guide you through the process of manifesting with emotion, helping you align your vision with the positive emotions that will anchor it in your mind and heart.

Your Turn

Take a moment to find a quiet space where you won't be disturbed. Close your eyes, relax, and allow yourself to fully engage with the guided visualisation video[62] below. Scan the QR code to access the video, and as you listen, focus on feeling your vision as well as seeing it.

Let those emotions energise your entire being.

PART 9

EMBRACING ABUNDANCE "LETLOTLO"

WHEN I WAS BORN, my mother named me *Letlotlo*, which translates to *Abundance* in English. As a young girl, I never fully grasped the significance of my name. It wasn't common, and it is often mispronounced. But now, as a grown woman reflecting on my life, I see how deeply meaningful my name truly is.

"Letlotlo" encapsulates the essence of abundance, both as a concept, and as a lived experience. My mother took the time to explain the significance of this name, often referring to the Bible, where Jesus says:

> *I have come that they may have life, and that they may have it more abundantly* (John 10:10).

The word *abundantly* in Greek, *Perissos*[63], suggests a life that goes beyond the ordinary, a life overflowing with joy, purpose, love, and fulfilment. The *Cambridge Dictionary* defines abundance as "*the quality of having what you want in life, such as love, happiness or career success*"[64]

In my culture, and according to the Bible, Letlotlo signifies a life of blessings, prosperity, and richness in every aspect. Understanding this, I realised that my mother had prophesied abundance into my life from the moment I was born. This prophecy has been a guiding force for me, shaping my actions, mindset, and overall approach to life.

Believing in abundance has transformed how I live. It's a reminder of the limitless growth and fulfilment that's possible when we embrace the abundance around us. And as you read on, I invite you to explore the richness of abundance in your own life.

Abundant Life

So, what is an abundant life, and how can you cultivate it? An abundant life is characterised by joy, optimism, purpose, and fulfilment. It's not just about material wealth; it extends to emotional, mental, and spiritual well-being.

Here are five key elements to help you cultivate an abundant life:

1. **Set Clear Goals**

   As discussed in the previous chapter on visualisation, having a roadmap to your abundant life is essential. Define what abundance means to you and set specific, measurable, achievable, relevant, and time-bound (SMART) goals to work towards your vision.

2. **Practice Gratitude**

   In positive psychology, gratitude is a powerful way to acknowledge the good in life. Psychologists Robert Emmons and Michael McCullough describe gratitude as "recognizing a positive outcome and understanding its external source"[65]. I struggled to find gratitude after losing my mother, but I realised that gratitude is not about being thankful all the time. It's about appreciating what the deceased gave us and how their influence continues to shape our lives. Keeping a gratitude journal can shift your mindset from scarcity to abundance.

3. **Foster Positive Relationships**

   Positive relationships are vital to our well-being and contribute to an abundant life. Dr Martin Seligman introduced the PERMA model in his book *Flourish: A Visionary New Understanding of Happiness and Wellbeing*.[66] One element of this model, "R," stands for Relationships. The quality of your relationships, whether familial, romantic, or professional, can significantly impact your sense of abundance. As human beings, the instinct to belong is deeply ingrained in us. It's a fundamental part of our nature, essential to our sense of identity and well-being. The connections we form with others play a crucial role in shaping the quality of our lives. Whether these relationships are familial, romantic, or professional, the people we surround ourselves with can either uplift us, filling our lives with joy and positive energy, or they can drain and damage us, leaving us feeling isolated and unhappy.

   Think about the different relationships you've had in your life. Some may have brought you happiness and energy, making you feel truly alive. Others, however, might have left you feeling depleted, even isolated, weighed down by sadness. The quality of these connections is vital, and recognising their impact is key to living a life of abundance and well-being.

My Story

In December 2023, I was filled with excitement at the thought of finally returning home to Botswana for Christmas. After battling cancer and enduring the isolating impact of the COVID-19 pandemic, I longed to be with my family. During those difficult times, travel restrictions made it impossible to be with loved ones in person, and we were left to rely on video calls to keep in touch. As COVID-19 slowly receded and travel restrictions were lifted, the opportunity to reunite with my family felt like a precious gift. I couldn't wait to see those who had survived the pandemic and to pay my respects to those who hadn't. The trip held special significance for me, especially because I was eager to visit my 94-year-old grandmother, who often asked when I would come home.

But what I hoped would be a joyous holiday turned out to be one of the most challenging times in my life.

One of the harshest lessons I learned during that holiday is that deception can be incredibly destructive within a family. No matter how long it takes, the truth always finds a way to come out, and when it does, it can leave behind a trail of brokenness. Trust, once corroded, is hard to rebuild. Trying to hide the truth only compounds the stress and pain, and it's a painful reality that openness and honesty are crucial for maintaining healthy family relationships. If something feels off, it's better to confront it early on. Bottling up your feelings only leads to division, gossip, lies, and more damage.

That holiday, which I now refer to as "unpleasant," taught me many things. I realised that when people are walking on eggshells, they are easily offended. Speaking the truth in such an environment often feels like opening a can of worms. People may go to great lengths to discredit you, recruiting others to their cause to divert attention from the real issues at hand.

Choosing Peace Over Toxicity

The moral of this story is simple but profound: if you find yourself exchanging more negative energy than positive in any relationship, there's no harm in maintaining a distance. If the relationship still holds value, you can relate from afar; if not, it might be best to cut ties altogether. That experience made me realise that peace is what I truly need. I'd rather have peace than maintain relationships that are built on gossip, lies, secrets, and deception.

I also came to understand my own imperfections in dealing with the situation, but I am grateful that I spoke the truth. It's vital to be conscious of how your relationships truly make you feel. Do they add to the quality of your life, or do they bring anxiety, stress, depression, sadness, and isolation?

Fostering Positive Relationships

The experience I went through taught me valuable lessons about fostering positive relationships. Here's what I learned:

1. **Improve Your Communication Skills**
   Reflecting on my story, I realised that the fire was sparked by a lack of proper communication. It's essential to give your undivided attention to the people you care about. This simple act shows that you genuinely care about them and the relationship. Improving your communication skills can bring people together and prevent misunderstandings before they escalate.

2. **Address Issues as They Arise**
   In all relationships, conflicts will arise from time to time. If I had addressed the issues I encountered while I was home, instead of returning to Ireland with unresolved feelings, the situation might not have escalated as it did.

Sometimes, resolving conflicts requires patience and understanding, but it's important for both parties to reach a consensus to restore the relationship. I eventually made peace with those who were willing, and I LET GO of the rest. As discussed in Part 1, letting go opened up space for abundance in my life.

3. **Focus on Positive Ideas and Common Ground**

   In any relationship, it's helpful to focus on what you have in common and to support each other's goals. Find out what the people you care about wish to accomplish and offer your support to help them achieve those goals. This mutual encouragement can strengthen your bonds and create a positive dynamic in your relationships.

4. **Remove Toxic Relationships From Your Life**

   To build healthy relationships, you need to invest effort, energy, and time. These are the relationships worth nurturing. However, it's equally important to CUT OUT relationships that no longer serve you. If a relationship consistently brings negativity into your life, it's okay to step away. Your peace and well-being are worth more than maintaining toxic connections.

My holiday trip to Botswana wasn't what I expected, but it taught me invaluable lessons about the importance of truth, communication, and choosing peace. In the end, I learnt that maintaining positive relationships requires effort, honesty, and sometimes, difficult choices. But it's these choices that allow us to cultivate a life filled with peace, authenticity, and abundance.

Embracing a Growth Mindset

Embracing a growth mindset is essential in achieving an abundant life because it fosters a belief in the potential for development and improvement in all areas of life. This type of mindset, coined by a Stanford University psychologist, Carol Dweck, contrasts a fixed mindset where individuals believe their abilities and traits are static. In her book *The Mindset: New Psychology of Success*[7], Dweck's research shows that our beliefs about our abilities and potential can profoundly influence how we behave, learn, and our overall satisfaction.

Embracing a positive mindset is a transformative practice that can empower you to face challenges with resilience, learn from every experience, and cultivate a life filled with joy and purpose. Here's how you can adopt and nurture a positive mindset:

1. **Embrace Challenges**

   One of the most powerful ways to cultivate a positive mindset is by embracing challenges, seeing them not as obstacles but as opportunities for growth. This process – known as positive reframing – helps shift your perspective, reducing the fear and anxiety often associated with difficult tasks.

   Let me share a personal experience:

   During the process of writing this book, I often felt overwhelmed. The sheer magnitude of the challenge I had set for myself sometimes felt insurmountable. There were moments when I questioned whether I had the strength and determination to see it through. The thought of giving up would creep in, sapping my energy and willpower. In those moments, I would pause and ask myself, "Why am I doing this? What is the deeper purpose behind sharing my story with the world?"

Answering this question, my "Why" always reignited my enthusiasm. It reminded me that this book was more than simply a personal project; it was a way to inspire, connect, and give hope to others. By reframing the challenge in this way, I transformed what seemed like a daunting task into a meaningful mission, empowering myself to keep writing, even when the journey was tough.

2. **Seek Learning Opportunities**

   Challenges often come with hidden gifts, learning opportunities that can enrich your life in unexpected ways. When I embarked on writing this book, I didn't just see it as a challenge; I saw it as a chance to learn and grow. The process required me to delve deep into research, explore new topics, and reflect on my own experiences in ways I hadn't before.

   Each moment of struggle became a learning experience. Embracing this growth mindset allowed me to see beyond the immediate difficulty and recognise the value in every step of the journey. It transformed the act of writing from a mere task into an exploration of knowledge and self-discovery. By seeing challenges as opportunities to learn, you too can turn daunting tasks into exciting adventures.

3. **Acknowledge and Challenge Fixed Mindset Thoughts**

   A key aspect of maintaining a positive mindset is becoming self-aware, recognising when you're slipping into a fixed mindset and challenging those limiting thoughts. A fixed mindset convinces you that your abilities and circumstances are static, that you can't grow or change. But this isn't true. By questioning the validity of these thoughts and replacing them with growth-oriented alternatives, you can break free from their constraints.

For example, when I found myself thinking, "I'm not cut out for writing a book," I challenged that thought by reminding myself of past accomplishments. I used positive affirmations to counteract negativity, affirming that I was capable of learning, growing, and succeeding. This practice of challenging and reframing fixed mindset thoughts is crucial in fostering a positive outlook and staying motivated.

4. **Persist in the Face of Setbacks**

   Persistence is a cornerstone of a growth mindset. When you encounter obstacles, a positive mindset encourages you to adapt and keep moving forward. Instead of viewing setbacks as failures, see them as opportunities to adjust your approach and learn new strategies. This resilience is what keeps you going when the road gets tough, ensuring that you don't just survive challenges, but thrive through them.

5. **Value Effort as a Path to Mastery**

   Understanding that effort is essential for improvement and success is vital in maintaining a positive approach to life. When you recognise that every ounce of effort brings you closer to mastery, you become more motivated to tackle challenges head-on. This belief in the value of effort reinforces the idea that success isn't about being naturally talented; it's about dedication, hard work, and a willingness to grow.

6. **Find Inspiration in Others' Success**

   Instead of seeing others' achievements as competition or a threat, use them as a source of inspiration and learning. Engage with people who have succeeded in areas you're passionate about and view their journeys as proof that success is possible. Collaborative learning, and sharing knowledge and experiences, can enhance your personal growth and positivity. Seeing others succeed should remind you that you too can achieve great things with the right mindset and effort.

7. **Pursue Passion and Creativity**

   Pursuing your passions and embracing creativity are integral to living an abundant, positive life. These pursuits bring intrinsic motivation, joy, and a sense of purpose. They're not simply hobbies; they're vital components of your well-being, enhancing your problem-solving abilities, personal expression, and overall happiness.

How can you integrate passion and creativity into your life?

Start by identifying your passions. Reflect on activities or interests that make you feel excited and fulfilled. Consider what you loved doing as a child or those moments when you lose track of time because you're so engrossed in an activity. Positive psychologist Mihaly Csikszentmihalyi describes this state of complete immersion as "flow."[67] Achieving this state of flow can significantly enhance your enjoyment, energy, and involvement in life.

Your Turn

Imagine for a moment an activity where your attention is fully focused, time flies by, and your whole being is engaged. What are you doing? What makes this activity so captivating?

For me, I enter this state of flow when I'm writing, reading, cooking, or playing chess. Whenever I engage in these activities, I feel highly interested, fully engaged, at peace, and calm. These moments are where I find true joy and fulfilment, and they remind me of the importance of nurturing my passions.

Achieving an abundant life is a continuous process of growth, self-discovery, and mindful living. This journey is rich with rewards, offering much more than material success. The true benefits of an abundant life are profound and multifaceted, encompassing emotional, physical, and spiritual well-being.

One of the most significant benefits is **happiness**. When you live abundantly, you cultivate a mindset that focuses on the positive aspects of life, embracing gratitude, joy, and contentment. This happiness is not fleeting; it's a deep-seated sense of satisfaction that permeates every aspect of your life, from your relationships to your daily activities.

Another vital aspect is **better health**. Abundance in life often leads to healthier choices, both physically and mentally. When you feel fulfilled and balanced, you're more likely to take care of your body through proper nutrition, exercise, and rest. Moreover, mental health improves as you foster positive thoughts and emotions, reducing stress and anxiety, which are common detractors of well-being.

Increased resilience is another key benefit. The journey to an abundant life teaches you to navigate challenges with grace and perseverance. Instead of viewing obstacles as insurmountable, you begin to see them as opportunities for growth. This shift in perspective makes you more resilient, able to bounce back from setbacks with a stronger, more positive outlook.

Greater productivity naturally follows. When you're living abundantly, you're aligned with your passions and purpose. This alignment fuels your motivation and energy, making you more effective and efficient in your pursuits. Whether in your career or personal projects, this heightened productivity stems from a place of enthusiasm and commitment, rather than obligation.

Lastly, **deeper fulfilment** is perhaps the most rewarding aspect of an abundant life. Fulfilment comes from living in accordance with your values, pursuing your passions, and contributing to something larger than yourself. It's the feeling that your life has meaning and purpose, that you're not simply going through the motions but truly living.

To create such a rich and satisfying existence, it's essential to focus on **holistic well-being**. This means nurturing all aspects of yourself: mind, body, and spirit. By integrating **passion, creativity, and generosity** into your daily life, you tap into your deepest desires and talents, which in turn fosters a sense of accomplishment and joy.

Passion drives you to pursue what you love, whether it's a career, a hobby, or a cause. It fuels your **creativity**, which allows you to think outside the box, solve problems in innovative ways, and express yourself authentically. **Generosity**, on the other hand, connects you with others, fostering a sense of community and shared purpose. When you give freely, whether it's your time, resources, or love, you create a ripple effect that positively impacts those around you, enhancing their lives as well as your own.

Ultimately, living an abundant life is about finding balance and harmony in all areas. It's about recognising that true wealth isn't only about what you have, but who you are and how you contribute to the world. As you focus on these aspects, you'll find that your life not only becomes more satisfying but also more impactful, leaving a legacy of abundance that touches everyone you encounter.

Abundant Healing

Abundant healing is a powerful concept that encapsulates the journey I've undertaken, one marked by resilience, faith, and the relentless pursuit of personal and professional growth, despite overwhelming challenges.

Surviving cancer in the middle of a global pandemic is an extraordinary testament to my strength and determination. This period was not simply about battling a severe illness; it was about confronting one of the most isolating and fear-inducing times in recent history. The pandemic added layers of complexity to my fight, with restricted access to physical support systems, heightened anxiety, and the constant backdrop of uncertainty. Yet, in the midst of this, I found the strength not only to survive but to thrive.

My story of abundant healing is deeply tied to my academic achievements during this time. Pursuing and achieving a first-class honours degree amidst such adversity is nothing short of remarkable. It speaks to a kind of healing that goes beyond the physical; it's about reclaiming my life, asserting my purpose, and proving to myself and the world that my spirit could not be broken. Graduating online, while not the traditional celebration, symbolises the triumph of human resilience and the ability to adapt and overcome even the most unexpected of circumstances.

This journey towards abundant healing was evident during one of the most transformative periods of my life. After months of intense struggle and uncertainty, I achieved a long-held goal by January 2021, a year after my surgery. I secured a position as one of the Clinical Leads in the Clinical Support Team at Ireland's largest COVID-19 Contact Tracing Centre. This office job was a dream I had been waiting for, a significant shift from the demanding world of bedside nursing.

I still remember the day I shared the good news with my therapist during one of our online sessions. Her face turned pale with concern as she gently reminded me, "COVID is still out there, and you're vulnerable." I could see her worry, but with tears welling up in my eyes, I spoke from my heart.

"Thank you for your concern," I said, "but this is an opportunity I've been waiting for for so long. Staying indoors alone has been its own challenge, and this office job, it's more than just a break from shift work. It's a chance to move forward."

My voice trembled as I remembered something that had stayed with me for years. When I first expressed my desire to transition from bedside nursing to an office job in Ireland, someone looked at me and said, "Not as a Black person. It's hard for 'us' to get office jobs. 'Our' work is to be carers, nurses, security guards, waiters, and childminders."

I recalled laughing and responding with boldness: "Watch me!"

As I sat there, sharing my joy with my therapist, those words echoed in my mind. Life doesn't always wait for you to be fully prepared when opportunities arise; it's up to you to recognise them, seize them, and run with them. And that's exactly what I did.

Taking on the role during the height of the pandemic was not easy, but I embraced the challenge. I thrived in the diversity of my team, united by a common purpose: to fight the pandemic and support those affected. I knew the risks, but I leaned into my faith, trusting that I was covered and protected. This role, though demanding, opened doors I had only dreamed of, and through it all, I remained healthy and COVID-free.

Even as I write these words, I reflect on the immense gratitude I carry for that chapter of my life. It wasn't simply about securing an office job; it was about defying expectations, stepping into my purpose, and trusting in the path that was meant for me. This milestone represents more than a career achievement; it's the culmination of a journey that started with survival and ended with thriving. It shows that my healing process was not passive but active and intentional. I chose to move forward, to set goals, and to achieve them despite the obstacles in my path. My ability to secure a job in a competitive field during such uncertain times is a clear indication that my healing has been both abundant and transformative.

My experience is a vivid illustration of how abundant healing is about more than just returning to a previous state of health or normalcy. It's about growing through the pain, finding new strengths, and emerging on the other side with a deeper understanding of yourself and your capabilities. I've shown that healing can lead to new beginnings, new achievements, and a life redefined by purpose and passion.

In essence, my journey embodies the idea that abundant healing is about thriving. It's about finding the courage to continue moving forward, even when the road is uncertain, and emerging from the storm with a renewed sense of purpose, strength, and possibility.

Post-Traumatic Growth: Blossoming After the Storm

"In this world, nothing is certain except death and taxes."

Benjamin Franklin (1706–1790)
American polymath, inventor, and Founding Father

Benjamin Franklin's words ring true, but one could argue that there's another certainty in life: at some point, everyone will experience a traumatic event. These events can hit like unrelenting storms, shaking the very foundations of our world and leaving behind a landscape of devastation.

What is Trauma?

The American Psychological Association (APA) defines trauma as "an emotional response to a terrible event."[68]

Traumatic events can take many forms, including sexual assault, especially in childhood, where vulnerable individuals are often targeted by those they trust. Fear, or the power dynamics involved, may keep victims silent, and when the perpetrator is a family member, the issue may be swept under the rug, leading to deep-seated scars that persist into adulthood. This is just one example of childhood trauma.

Other traumatic experiences include life-threatening illnesses, car accidents, raising a child with a severe condition, enduring the horrors of war, surviving a global pandemic, losing a loved one, or going through a divorce. Natural disasters – like earthquakes, the loss of a job, and countless other life-altering events – can leave lasting impacts on our emotional, mental, and physical well-being.

Yet, while trauma is a universal experience, how we respond to it is deeply personal. Each of us perceives and processes these events in our own unique way.

Below is a list of effects of trauma on individuals adopted from psychologist Richard G. Tedeschi and Bret A. Moore's book, *The Post-Traumatic Growth Workbook.* [69]

- Helplessness
- Memory loss
- Feeling hopeless
- Feeling alone
- Feeling afraid
- Disorientation
- Anger
- Anxiety and panic
- Crying
- Headaches
- Withdrawal from others
- Distractibility
- Nausea and vomiting
- Nightmares

- Thoughts about death and dying
- Lack of confidence
- Feeling sad
- Fatigue and tiredness
- Obsessive thoughts
- Frustration
- Increased sleeping
- Racing heart
- Diarrhoea
- Arguing with loved ones
- Confusion
- Increased drug and alcohol use
- Hot flushes
- Shakiness and trembling
- Loss of concentration
- Impulsive behaviour
- Lack of confidence
- Changes in appetite
- Aggression
- Feeling numb
- Aches and pains

Your Turn

Before I move on to discuss the aftermath of traumatic experiences, I would like you to complete an exercise below. Identify a traumatic experience you had – there may be two or more but there is one that had a greater impact on you.

Tedeschi and Moore (see above) came up with this exercise so that you can identify the symptoms you experienced. This exercise will then help you to normalise what you went through and its effects. You can use the space provided here or write your answers in your journal if you would prefer.

____

____

____

____

____

____

My Story

The harrowing experiences of losing loved ones and facing a life-threatening illness are often seen as the lowest points in life. Throughout this book, I have shared my journey through these traumatic events. The trauma began during the two weeks I spent visiting my mother at one of Botswana's largest referral hospitals. During this time, I witnessed the care she received, which was deeply distressing and far from what anyone should experience. I had paused my internship to be by her side, hoping for better days, but instead, I found myself facing a painful reality. What shook me to my core was arriving at the hospital to find my mother abandoned in a corner. She was frail, unable to eat or walk, lying helplessly in a sunken bed. To make matters worse, on several occasions, my family was informed that she had missed her cancer treatment because no ambulance was available to transport her to the treatment centre. The scene that greeted me was nothing short of heartbreaking; she was being wheeled around in a makeshift wheelchair, essentially a garden chair mounted on bicycle rims. It had no cushioning, no brakes, and no protective belt. The sight sent chills down my spine, and to this day, that haunting image lingers in my mind, overshadowing even the pain of her passing. It was horrific.

Despite the overwhelming trauma, something began to shift within me over time. While I experienced many of the trauma symptoms I've mentioned earlier, I also started to notice a change in how I saw myself and how I approached life. It's common to focus on the negative outcomes of trauma, but what about the positive ones? Do they even exist? This is where the concept of post-traumatic growth comes in. It suggests that positive personal changes can emerge in the aftermath of trauma.

A couple of years after losing my mother, my friend, and losing a breast to cancer, I struggled to cope and move forward. The losses were heavy, but gradually, I began to develop a deeper sense of self-awareness. Research shows that people with strong self-awareness tend to have a more positive outlook on life and are often more compassionate towards themselves and others. Self-awareness brought clarity to my situation, helping me find balance, contentment, resilience, and wisdom.

In addition to this transformation, I discovered a deeper sense of spiritual growth. I remember praying fervently for God to save me, to heal me, and to give me the strength to get back on track, to live my life fully, and reach my destiny. This journey has been challenging, but it has also led me to a place of profound personal and spiritual growth.

Let's delve deeper into the concept of post-traumatic growth (PTG) through the lens of positive psychology. I've read books about people who found meaning and purpose in their lives after enduring traumatic events, but I was unaware of the term "post-traumatic growth" until one of my lecturers introduced it to us in class. Dr Jolanta Burke – an expert in positive psychology and co-author of *Positive Health: 100+ Research-based Positive Psychology and Lifestyle Medicine Tools to Enhance Your Wellbeing*[70], a book I highly recommend – was the one who opened my eyes to this phenomenon. The concept immediately resonated with me, as it reflected the transformations I've experienced since going through trauma, and it helped explain why these changes often lead to a renewed sense of meaning and purpose in life.

As I mentioned earlier, trauma can create prolonged stress, leading to an imbalance in our physical, emotional, and psychological well-being. However, research suggests that stress can have beneficial effects, provided it isn't prolonged. Psychologists Boniwell and Tunariu have pointed out that encountering adversity or trauma can equip us with "psychological preparedness," allowing us to become stronger. Research shows that while 5–35% of people may succumb to trauma and end up in a negative emotional state, positive psychology asks an intriguing question: What about the other 65–95%?

In their book *Positive Psychology: Theory, Research and Applications*,[71] Boniwell and Tunariu outline three possible outcomes that can result from trauma:

1. Succumbing to the stressor
2. Bouncing back from stress – a resilience-focused recovery
3. Sustainable recovery, leading to growth and enhancement – Post-Traumatic Growth (PTG)

In this chapter, I'll focus on the third outcome: post-traumatic growth, a concept first identified in the mid-1990s by psychologists Richard Tedeschi and Lawrence Calhoun.[72] They define PTG as the positive psychological changes that can occur when an individual struggles with and overcomes adversity. They explored this phenomenon further, identifying five domains of growth, measured by what they called the Post-Traumatic Growth Inventory (PTGI).

The first domain is a **change in relationships**, specifically, the ability to form deeper connections with others while also identifying those who truly support us in times of need. Life's inevitable challenges act as a crucible, revealing the true nature of those around us. The genuine character, intentions, and loyalty of people are brought to light during these times. Recognising these "true colours" helps us to nurture and cherish relationships that uplift us while distancing ourselves from those that do not contribute positively to our lives.

For anyone who has gone through difficult times, this probably sounds familiar. I know it resonates deeply with my own experience, which I'm about to share with you.

I firmly believe that everyone we meet has a role to play in our lives, particularly during the different seasons we go through. I believe that God places the right people in our path for a purpose, and even the wrong ones to teach us valuable lessons. I have been blessed with people who have played generous roles in my life at various times. Among these people are my family, friends, and even strangers. Out of all these connections, there are a few friends I hold close to my heart, especially those who were there for me when my mother passed away and when I was diagnosed with cancer.

One friend in particular, Miriam, has been by my side through thick and thin, even before these two most traumatic events. She has been there for me, even when I relocated to Ireland and was scammed by two con artists. From the beginning of our friendship, Miriam took the time to get to know me, and the feeling was mutual. She quickly became more than a friend; she became family. My mother knew her, and I grew close to her family and children as well. We've supported each other in times of need, and she's the first person I call whenever I face challenges. She's always there, without judgement, ready to listen and help. Of course, we've had our differences, but that's normal; it's part of being human. What matters is that we always find a way to resolve any conflict amicably. These are the kinds of relationships worth keeping, the ones that are supportive, positive, and full of good energy.

Life has a way of revealing its deepest truths during our most challenging times. In 2015, when my mother fell ill and eventually passed away, I found myself in one of those defining seasons. It was a time of intense grief and heartache, but it was also a time of revelation, a season that exposed the true nature of the friendships I had cultivated over the years. I learned then, as I would again during my own health struggles after surgery, that some people are placed in our lives by God for a specific season and a specific purpose.

Some friends stood by me unwaveringly, offering support, comfort, and understanding. These were the ones who didn't shy away from the uncomfortable reality of illness and loss. They were there to hold my hand, listen to my pain, and simply be present when words failed. Others, however, faded away, unable or unwilling to walk alongside me in my grief. It was a painful realisation, but one that taught me an invaluable lesson: not everyone is meant to stay in your life forever, and that's okay.

This lesson was reinforced during my own health struggles after surgery. The COVID-19 pandemic added an extra layer of isolation to an already difficult experience. Much of my healing process was spent alone, physically distant from the very people who might have offered support in a different time. Yet even in that solitude, there were those who found ways to reach out, to check in, to offer their love and prayers from afar. These friendships were the lifelines God provided for that specific season, offering the emotional and spiritual strength I needed to get through those dark days, even if their presence was sometimes only felt through a phone call or a message.

As I began to recover and regain my strength, something unexpected happened: some of those friendships that had been so vital during my illness began to fade away. They ended abruptly, without explanation, leaving me with a sense of confusion and unanswered questions. Why would these relationships, which had been so important during my darkest hours, suddenly disappear just as I was beginning to see the light again?

It took time, reflection, and prayer to come to terms with this new reality. I came to understand that everyone has a role to play in our lives, but not everyone is meant to stay forever. Some people are sent to us for a specific purpose, to help us through a particular season, and once that purpose is fulfilled, they move on. It's a difficult truth to accept, especially when we've grown attached to these individuals, but it's a truth that has brought me peace. Rather than focusing on the relationships that ended, I chose to focus on my own healing journey and the goals I had set for myself.

After my recovery, I made a promise to myself, and to God, that I would soar like an eagle, rising above the challenges and becoming the best version of myself. This promise became the driving force behind my actions and decisions. I channelled my energy into healing, not only physically, but emotionally and spiritually as well.

I remember watching a YouTube video by Tony Robbins, the famous American author, coach, and speaker, where he said, "Where focus goes, energy flows."[73] This is a powerful reminder that our attention and thoughts shape our reality. When you direct your focus towards something, whether it's a goal, a dream, or even a challenge, your energy naturally follows, fuelling your actions and decisions. This means that by consciously choosing where to place your focus, you can drive progress and bring about the changes you desire in your life.

If you focus on positivity, growth, and opportunities, you'll find yourself moving towards them with greater determination. Conversely, if your focus is on fear, doubt, or obstacles, that's where your energy will go, potentially creating more of what you don't want.

The key to this principle is mindfulness – being aware of where your focus is at any given moment and actively choosing to direct it towards what empowers and uplifts you. By harnessing this power, you can channel your energy into creating the life you envision.

As I began to redefine my life, I set new goals and pursued them with the same determination that had carried me through my illness. This journey wasn't always easy. There were moments when I felt the weight of lost relationships, and the absence of those who had once been close to me was deeply felt. But instead of dwelling on what was no longer there, I chose to focus on the blessings that remained. I practiced gratitude for those who had been part of my life during those challenging times, recognising that their presence, no matter how brief, played a crucial role in my journey.

They were there when I needed them most, and for that, I was deeply thankful. Whether they stood by me only for a season or remained as I soared to new heights, each person left an indelible mark on my heart. Their support, love, and even their departure shaped me into who I am today. I've come to believe that everyone we encounter plays a role in our lives. Some are here to teach us lessons, others to provide support, and still others to help us grow in ways we never imagined. Not all of them will stay, but their impact endures.

This understanding has allowed me to let go of the pain of lost friendships and instead focus on the positive contributions they made during the time they were in my life. I carry with me the lessons from those past seasons, and I'm more focused than ever on becoming the best version of myself, living out the promise I made to God. Life is full of seasons, each with its own challenges, joys, and cast of characters. Some will walk with us only a short distance, while others will stay for the long haul. But in every season, there is a purpose, and in every ending, there is a new beginning.

My focus is no longer on what has been lost but on what lies ahead. The relationships that ended were a part of my journey, but they do not define it. What defines my journey is the strength I've found, the goals I've achieved, and the promise I've kept to myself and to God. I will continue to soar, to grow, and to embrace each new season with an open heart, grateful for all that has been and all that is yet to come.

Rather than being solely defined by the pain of the past, post-traumatic growth (PTG) offers a sense of renewed purpose and possibility. PTG is about discovering new strengths, perspectives, and opportunities that may not have been visible before the trauma. Embracing life's possibilities in the context of PTG means recognising that, even after deep pain or loss, new adventures await. This might involve a shift in career or the pursuit of passions that bring fulfilment. It's the realisation that, while trauma changes you, it also opens doors to growth, resilience, and a life re-imagined with greater meaning and potential.

During the healing process following my trauma, I was also pursuing my second degree in Marketing, Digital Media, and Cloud Computing. My focus at that time was to advance in the field of technology, a sector that fascinated me and promised a future full of possibilities. This passion led me to enrol in a master's program in Business Analytics, a logical next step in my career progression. However, as I journeyed through this academic path, my health challenges became increasingly demanding, and I made the difficult decision to step away from the program.

Taking a year off was not part of my original plan, but during this period of reflection and recovery, I began to sense a deeper redirection in my life. I realised that the trauma I had endured was not merely a setback; it was a catalyst for transformation. In the midst of my struggles, I found myself being gently nudged towards a new path, one that aligned with a more profound sense of purpose. It became clear to me that my true calling lay not only in advancing in technology, but in using my experiences to help and inspire others.

This realisation was further solidified when I came across Doug D. Gordon's book, *Charge Yourself Up for Success*[74]. Gordon, an international award winner, author, speaker, and coach, offers powerful insights on how to navigate life's challenges and turn them into opportunities for growth. In one of the chapters, he speaks about "turning your mess into a message and giving it meaning." This concept resonated deeply with me. I had always wanted to write a book in honour of my mother and the wisdom she instilled in me, but it was the reflection on the "mess" I had been through in the past years that truly fuelled my desire to bring this book to life.

The experiences I've navigated through – the pain, the healing, the moments of doubt – have all become integral parts of my story. They have shaped who I am today and have given me a new mission: to share these experiences with others. By completing this book, I aim to offer hope and inspiration to anyone facing their own adversities, showing them that even in the darkest of times, there is a way forward. This journey has taught me that our greatest struggles can often lead us to our true purpose, and it is my hope that by sharing my story, I can help others find meaning in their own challenges and emerge stronger on the other side.

After enduring years of trauma and hardship, I found myself at a crossroads, seeking a new direction that would not only heal me but also align with my deeper sense of purpose. It was during this period of reflection and re-evaluation that I made a pivotal decision to enrol in a Master of Science in Positive Health Coaching with the Royal College of Surgeons in Ireland.

This was not simply an academic pursuit; it was a step towards transforming my life and the lives of others. This master's program has been instrumental in equipping me with evidence-based resources that enhance my understanding of the critical role our behaviour plays in optimising health and well-being. Through this education, I've learned how to integrate the emerging scientific discipline of positive psychology into the realms of lifestyle and integrative medicine. The program has provided me with a comprehensive understanding of how our thoughts, behaviours, and choices directly influence our overall health, both physically and mentally.

Positive health coaching is about more than guiding others towards healthier habits; it's about empowering individuals to take control of their lives by fostering a mindset that encourages growth, resilience, and positive change. The integration of positive psychology within this framework is particularly powerful, as it emphasises the importance of mental and emotional well-being in achieving overall health. This holistic approach resonated with me deeply, especially given my own experiences with trauma and healing.

As I progressed through the program, I began to see how the various threads of my life were coming together. The trauma I had endured, which once felt like an insurmountable "mess," began to reveal itself as a source of strength and insight. My years of nursing experience, coupled with the leadership skills I had developed, provided a solid foundation on which to build this new phase of my life. Positive health coaching became the bridge that connected my past experiences with my future aspirations.

I realised that my story, with all its pain and resilience, had the potential to become a powerful message for others. The journey from trauma to healing, from uncertainty to purpose, is one that many people can relate to. By combining my personal experiences with the knowledge and skills I've gained through positive health coaching, I now have the tools to help others navigate their own challenges and discover their own paths to well-being.

It may sound strange to some, but I find myself grateful for everything I've been through. Each hardship, each setback, has played a crucial role in redirecting me towards a life filled with purpose and meaning. The struggles that once seemed overwhelming have now become the foundation of my mission to inspire and uplift others. Through this book, I hope to share the lessons I've learned, the insights I've gained, and the strategies that have helped me transform my life. My goal is not just to tell my story but to use it as a vehicle for spreading messages of hope, resilience, and the power of positive health. I want to inspire you to see your own challenges as opportunities for growth, to understand that even in the darkest of times, there is a way forward. By turning my "mess" into a message, I aim to contribute to your life, especially if you're struggling, by offering the encouragement and guidance you need to find your own sense of purpose and well-being.

Tedeschi and Moore give an example of a young woman who was an athlete training to compete at Olympic level, her lifelong dream. Tragically, she was involved in a car accident that left her with a disability. Though devastated, she didn't give up on her dream but decided to compete as a Paralympic athlete instead. As she rehabilitated, something remarkable happened: her mindset shifted. Seeing others struggle in rehabilitation, she felt a new sense of purpose in helping and motivating them. Her original goal changed, but it was the trauma that redirected her towards a new path, a path with a different, yet equally meaningful, destination.

Similarly, the challenges I've faced have transformed my goals and life path, leading me to a purpose that I had never imagined. And it is with this new-found purpose that I now seek to inspire others to find meaning and growth in their own lives, no matter the adversity they face.

The Spiritual Awakening Through Trauma: My Journey

One of the most profound aspects of post-traumatic growth (PTG) is the **spiritual change** that often emerges from deep struggle. It is in those moments when we grapple with the meaning of our pain that we frequently find ourselves with a transformed perspective on life, a deepened spirituality, and a clearer sense of purpose.

My own journey through trauma led me to a place of spiritual awakening, one that has fundamentally changed how I live and perceive the world around me. I vividly remember the moment I reached out to God, pleading for healing. To my amazement, I found myself recovering without significant physical complications. As I bounced back from those harrowing experiences, I began to notice a shift in my perspective. Life took on a new hue, and I became acutely aware of the fragility of existence and the grace that sustains it.

As I navigated this spiritual transformation, I began to devote more of my life to seeking guidance from the Bible. This process helped me better understand my mother's deep spirituality. Growing up, she had always been devoted to her faith, raising us in the church, encouraging us to read the Bible, and teaching us to pray. At the time, I didn't fully grasp the depth of her commitment. But now, as I reflect on my own experiences, I realise that her spiritual dedication was likely shaped by the traumas she had endured throughout her life.

After my mother passed away, my siblings entrusted me with her Bible, a deeply personal and sacred object that she had cherished throughout her life. This Bible has since become a profound point of connection between my mother, myself, and Jesus Christ. It is from this Bible that I draw strength and solace, especially during moments of uncertainty.

There is something uniquely powerful about my mother's Bible. I've developed a habit of opening it randomly, allowing my mood to guide me to a particular verse. Time and time again, I find myself landing on passages that she had highlighted, verses that seem to speak directly to whatever situation I'm facing at that moment. The first time this happened, I was overwhelmed with emotion. The verse that appeared was:

> *But those who hope in the Lord will renew their strength. They will soar on wings like eagles; they will run and not grow weary; they will walk and not faint.* (Isaiah 40:31)

This verse brought me to tears, resonating deeply with the struggles I was enduring at that time. It felt as if my mother, through her highlighted scripture, was offering me a message of hope and encouragement from beyond. I clung to this teaching, believing in the abundance of strength and health that only God can provide.

Since then, my priorities and beliefs have undergone a significant transformation. I now put God first in everything I do, understanding Him as my Alpha and Omega, the first and the last (Revelation 22:13). This spiritual grounding has instilled in me a profound sense of calm and a reservoir of positive energy. I face each day with the knowledge that I can do all things through Christ who strengthens me (Philippians 4:13).

This spiritual journey, born out of trauma and shaped by faith, has not only brought me closer to God, but has also deepened my connection to my mother and the teachings she passed down to me. It has given me a renewed sense of purpose and a mission to share my story with others, to offer hope and inspiration.

One of the most impactful books I've read during this journey is *The Monk Who Sold His Ferrari* by Robin Sharma[10]. This book beautifully illustrates how PTG can lead to profound personal transformation, a re-evaluation of life's priorities, and a deeper sense of purpose. The story follows Julian Mantle, a successful but deeply unhappy lawyer who experiences a life-threatening heart attack. This event forces him to question the value of his material success and to search for a more meaningful existence. He travels to India, where he learns from the Sages of Sivana and discovers the secrets to a fulfilled, purposeful life.

Julian's traumatic experience compels him to abandon his former life and embrace a spiritual path that is more rewarding. Through this fictional tale, Sharma provides a roadmap for turning adversity into opportunities for growth, emphasising the power of mindfulness, meditation, and positive thinking in cultivating mental and emotional resilience.

Like Julian Mantle, my own journey has been one of profound transformation. The trauma I experienced pushed me to seek a deeper understanding of life and led me to a spiritual awakening that has reshaped my priorities and my purpose. Through this awakening, I've discovered the strength and resilience that come from faith, and I now strive to share these lessons with others, hoping to inspire them to find their own paths to healing and growth.

The fourth domain of post-traumatic growth (PTG) is **The Appreciation of Life**, and it's a shift in perspective that resonates deeply with those who have faced near-death experiences. You've likely heard people say, "Thank God for giving me a second chance to live," after surviving a brush with death. This phrase has become a part of my own vocabulary since my experience with cancer. The mere fact that I wake up each morning fills me with a gratitude that I had never fully understood before.

Near-death experiences have a unique way of stripping away the trivial concerns that once dominated our minds. They bring into sharp focus the simple gift of life itself. I began to notice this shift in myself, where the little things that once kept me awake at night, the worries about the future, the constant overthinking, started to lose their hold on me. I realised that these worries, no matter how persistent, do not change anything; they only rob us of our peace.

The world experienced a collective trauma with the arrival of COVID-19, a storm that swept through our lives and proved how quickly everything can change. The pandemic brought with it a stark reminder of life's fragility. People lost their loved ones, their livelihoods, and for many, their sense of security. Yet, amidst the chaos, a common thread emerged: a renewed appreciation for life. Priorities shifted, and suddenly, the small moments such as waking up each day, breathing freely, and spending time with loved ones, became the focal point of our existence.

My own traumatic experiences have dramatically altered my perspective on life. The future, once a source of constant anxiety, has become something I approach with a new-found sense of calm. I have trained my mind to embrace positivity, to be vigilant when negative thoughts begin to creep in. It's a practice, a discipline, that I've developed out of necessity, but it has transformed the way I live.

This shift didn't happen overnight. It was a gradual process, one that required me to confront the fears and anxieties that had been ingrained in me for so long. I had to learn to let go of the need to control every aspect of my life, to release the constant worry about what might happen tomorrow. Instead, I began to focus on the present moment, on the blessings that each day brings.

Appreciating life in its simplest form has become my mantra. I've come to understand that every breath, every sunrise, every smile, is a gift, one that should never be taken for granted. This perspective has given me a sense of peace that I never knew was possible, a peace that comes from accepting life as it is, with all its uncertainties and imperfections.

The trauma, the pain, the fear: they were all part of a process that ultimately led me to a deeper understanding of what it means to truly live. I've come to see that life's greatest challenges often carry within them the seeds of our most profound growth.

My hope is that by sharing my story, I can inspire you to find your own sense of appreciation for life, even in the face of adversity. We all face challenges, but it's how we respond to them that defines our journey.

In general, it's not about what we have or what we achieve, but about how we live each day, with gratitude, with purpose, and with an unwavering appreciation for the gift of life. After everything I've been through, I've come to understand that the love I once sought outside of myself has always existed within me. This realisation has transformed the way I live and interact with the world.

Trauma has a way of stripping us down to our core, exposing our vulnerabilities and weaknesses. It forces us to confront parts of ourselves we may have neglected or ignored. For years, I was so focused on the external – seeking validation, love, and approval from others – that I lost sight of the most important relationship I'll ever have: the one with myself. As I began to heal from my experiences, I came to understand that true self-love isn't about striving for perfection or pretending to have all the answers. It's about embracing who I am, fully and completely, including the visible scars that mark my body. These scars tell the story of my journey. They are reminders of the battles I've fought and the resilience I've shown in the face of adversity. For a long time, I struggled with these marks, viewing them as imperfections, as symbols of pain and suffering. But as I delved deeper into my healing process, I began to see them differently.

Accepting my scars was not simply about acknowledging the physical changes in my body; it is about embracing the emotional and spiritual transformation they represent. These scars are a testament to my strength, a visible narrative of survival. They are not flaws to be hidden or erased; they are parts of me that deserve love and respect. I am sure you can relate to this. Let your scars be a constant reminder of the strength you carry and the resilience that defines you. They are proof that you survived, that you faced adversity head-on and emerged stronger. My story is a testament to this truth, and I hope it inspires you to see your own scars, whether visible or hidden as badges of honour. Embrace them, for they are part of the powerful narrative of your life, a narrative of survival and strength.

In learning to love myself, I realised that self-love is much more than simply loving the parts of ourselves that are easy to accept. It's about finding compassion for the parts that we may have been taught to hide or feel ashamed of.

This acceptance wasn't instantaneous – it was a gradual process, one that required me to shift my perspective from seeing my scars as symbols of defeat to viewing them as badges of honour. Each scar represents a moment when I could have given up, but chose to keep fighting instead. When I look in the mirror, I now see a body that has been through the fire and emerged stronger. The scars no longer evoke feelings of loss or sadness; instead, they remind me of how far I've come. They are a part of my story, and I wouldn't be who I am today without them. The love that I had been searching for, the comfort and security I thought only others could provide, I discovered within myself. It was a powerful and liberating realisation. I no longer needed to chase after external sources of validation or affection. Instead, I began to nurture and cherish the love I have for myself.

This shift in perspective has had an impact on my life. It has allowed me to set healthy boundaries, to say no when I need to, and to prioritise my own well-being without guilt. I've learned that self-love isn't selfish; it's essential. It's about recognising your worth and treating yourself with the kindness and compassion you deserve. I've also discovered that self-love is a journey, not a destination. It's an ongoing practice that requires patience, effort, and a willingness to grow. Some days are easier than others, but even on the hardest days, remind yourself of how far you've come and the strength it took to get here.

Devoting your life to self-love brings a sense of peace and fulfilment that you never thought possible. It allows you to approach life with a renewed sense of confidence and purpose. You no longer feel the need to prove yourself to others or seek out their approval. You are enough, just as you are, and that's more than enough. The love we seek is already within us. It's up to us to embrace it, nurture it, and allow it to guide us on our journey. Through self-love, we can find healing, purpose, and a deeper connection to the life we've been given.

The last and most profound aspect of post-traumatic growth (PTG) is **the discovery and recognition of personal strengths**. This domain, perhaps more than any other, reveals the unexpected gifts that can emerge from the most challenging experiences.

I want you to take a moment and think about your own strengths. If I were to ask you to pause right now and write down five of your main personal strengths in your notebook, you might find yourself hesitating. You might second-guess yourself, wondering if the qualities you possess are truly strengths or simply aspects of your personality. It's a common reaction. We often struggle to see the value in ourselves, especially when life has tried to convince us otherwise.

But here's the thing: trauma has a way of revealing strengths we never knew we had. It's in the moments of greatest adversity that our true character is forged. The strengths we discover in these times aren't theoretical; they're real, tested, and proven in the fires of our experiences.

This domain of PTG highlights the changes that occur as individuals navigate through and emerge from trauma. Survivors often report feeling more confident, creative, resilient, and authentic than they did before their traumatic experiences. These aren't just words; they are reflections of deep, personal growth.

Confidence is one of the most significant shifts. After surviving trauma, you may find that you are surer of yourselves, as you may have faced the worst, and you've come out on the other side. This new-found confidence isn't based on arrogance or bravado. It's rooted in the knowledge that you have the inner strength to handle whatever comes your way. You've been tested, and you've passed.

Creativity also often flourishes in the aftermath of trauma. The process of healing can unlock parts of the mind that were previously dormant. You may find yourselves exploring new hobbies, engaging in artistic endeavours, or solving problems in innovative ways. This creative energy isn't simply a distraction from pain; it's a vital part of the healing process. It's a way of expressing the inexpressible, of turning pain into something beautiful and meaningful.

Resilience, of course, is another cornerstone of post-traumatic growth. The ability to bounce back, to keep moving forward even when it feels impossible, is a strength that many survivors develop. This resilience isn't about being invincible; it's about knowing that you can be knocked down and still find the strength to stand back up. It's about perseverance and the quiet determination that comes from having faced adversity before.

Finally, **authenticity** often emerges as a key strength. After experiencing trauma, you may find that you no longer have the energy or desire to pretend to be something you're not. You may have faced your deepest fears, and in doing so, you've stripped away the layers of pretence. What's left is a more authentic self, someone who is true to their own values and beliefs. This authenticity is a powerful strength, one that allows you to live more fully and honestly.

In the depths of my journey through trauma, I came to appreciate something that I had never fully understood before: the **profound strength that lies within us**, waiting to be discovered. This is one of the core aspects of post-traumatic growth (PTG), a domain that, like many, I initially struggled to grasp. Trauma had left me questioning everything, especially my own abilities. I wondered if I would ever feel strong again, if I would ever trust in my decisions, or if I would always be overshadowed by doubt.

But as I began to heal, I noticed subtle but powerful changes. I found myself growing more confident in my decisions, more creative in finding solutions to the problems life threw my way, and more resilient in the face of new challenges. Most importantly, I became more authentic, truer to myself. The layers of fear and uncertainty that once obscured my sense of self were gradually stripped away, revealing a person I hadn't fully recognised before, a person of strength, resilience, and deep inner resolve.

This chapter isn't just about my story; it's about you, too. It's an invitation to recognise and embrace your own strengths. You may not see them clearly right now, and that's okay. Growth takes time, and often, our strengths are revealed gradually, through the process of living and enduring. But they are there, waiting to be discovered, as mine were.

As a cancer survivor, I never would have imagined the depth of my internal strength had I not gone through the diagnosis. We all go about life knowing that something bad could happen, but often, it feels like those traumatic events are things that happen to other people, not to us. Then, when trauma does strike, we are forced to confront it head-on. It's in these moments that we discover a strength we never knew we had or perhaps never needed before.

I used to think that if my mother passed away, I would not be able to carry on with life. I believed my purpose was to reward her for being such a wonderful mother, to make her happy and proud of my achievements. When she succumbed to cancer, my world felt like it had shattered. But instead of breaking me, this loss contributed to a profound realisation of my own personal strengths. I learned that I could live and rely on myself, that I could face hardships, even ones I never imagined I'd have to endure.

It wasn't easy. It took time to accept things the way they were, to cope with the loss. But over time, I came to understand that being angry, resentful, or depressed over things I couldn't control was a waste of my precious time and energy. My mother's passing had, in its own painful way, prepared me for the battles that lay ahead, including my own fight against breast cancer, which came four years after her death.

Little did I know that the growth in my personal strength following my mother's death was fortifying me for what was to come. When I was diagnosed with breast cancer, right in the middle of the COVID-19 pandemic, I found myself facing yet another formidable challenge. I was in the middle of my final year exams, a period that would have been stressful under any circumstances, but the isolation and fear brought on by the pandemic made it even more so.

But I had something powerful to draw on, a reservoir of personal strength that I had been unknowingly building over the years. This reservoir is something we all have, though we might not realise it until we need it most. During challenging times, I reached into this reservoir, and it was there for me when I faced my illness.

I remember the day before one of my exams, an online exam due to COVID-19 restrictions. I was in a terrible state, overwhelmed by excruciating pain from the wound on my lower abdomen, the donor site for my breast reconstruction. The pain was aggravated by stress, anxiety, and hours of studying. I felt myself breaking down, tears streaming down my face as I felt hope and strength slipping away.

But then, I remembered my reservoir of personal strength. In that moment of desperation, I reached for my mother's photo. I turned it over and began to write on the back,

> *Dear Mum,*
>
> *I think I am losing my strength. Please, please strengthen me. I am nearly at the finish line. We can do this! You have been doing it for me, and I know you can do it for me again.*

I signed and dated it, and as I held that photo, I felt a shift within me.

The energy in the room changed. The confidence, determination, and motivation that had been slipping away came rushing back. The pain that had felt so overwhelming became numb, a background noise that I could push through. I went through that exam period with my reservoir of strength beside me, drawing on it day by day until the exams were over.

When I finally received my results, I had achieved a first-class degree, even in the midst of all the adversity I faced. This was more than simply an academic achievement; it was proof of the strength I had found within myself, a strength I might never have discovered without the trials I had endured.

This reservoir of personal strength is something we all have, something you can build and draw from in your own times of need. It's not about being invincible; it's about knowing that, no matter what happens, you have the strength within you to survive, to push through, and to emerge stronger on the other side.

So, as you face your own challenges, remember this: you have a reservoir of strength within you, waiting to be tapped into. And when you need it most, it will be there, just as it was for me. Before I share with you what's in my reservoir of personal strengths, take a moment to reflect on your journey in your notebook. Think about the challenges you've faced and how you've responded to them. Consider the ways in which you've grown, the strengths that have emerged from your struggles. These are the qualities that make you who you are, the strengths that will carry you forward into whatever comes next.

Call to Action

Here are some questions from Tedeschi and Calhoun from *The Post-Traumatic Growth Workbook*, which may guide you to appreciate your own personal strength and growth since trauma. Write the answers in your notebook.

1. What have you done to cope that most clearly demonstrates the strength that has got you through this difficult time?

____

____

____

____

2. What are some things that seemed difficult before trauma that now seem relatively easy for you, given what you have been through?

3. What advice might you have for others who think that a situation similar to yours is too difficult to manage?

As promised, here is **The Reservoir of My Personal Strengths**. I call it a reservoir, but you can call it a bag or give it any name that resonates with you. What is in my bag?

Resilience

This is one of those qualities that we often admire in others but may not fully recognise in ourselves until we are tested. It's the ability to bounce back from setbacks, to adapt to changing circumstances, and to keep moving forward even when life throws its hardest punches. Resilience isn't about never feeling pain or doubt; it's about finding the strength to rise again, time after time.

In my journey, resilience has been both a challenge and a gift. When I first faced my cancer diagnosis, it felt like the ground beneath me had disappeared. The future I had envisioned seemed uncertain, and every day brought new fears and challenges. But what I came to realise was that resilience isn't about avoiding these difficult emotions; it's about allowing yourself to feel them, process them, and then find a way to move forward.

Resilience is like a muscle; the more you use it, the stronger it becomes. Each setback I encountered – whether it was related to my health, personal loss, or even professional challenges – gave me an opportunity to exercise this muscle. I learned to adapt, to adjust my expectations, and to find new ways to approach the obstacles in my path. Sometimes, this meant taking small steps when larger ones felt impossible. Other times, it meant reaching out for support, knowing that resilience doesn't mean going it alone.

One of the most important lessons I've learned about resilience is that it's not only about bouncing back; it's about bouncing forward. It's about using each setback as a stepping stone, gaining strength and wisdom along the way. When I look back at the challenges I've faced, I see not only the pain and struggle but also the growth, the lessons learned, and the person I've become as a result.

Resilience has also taught me the importance of flexibility. Life rarely goes according to plan, and sometimes, the best thing we can do is adapt to new circumstances. Whether it's finding new ways to pursue our goals or adjusting our expectations when things don't turn out as expected, resilience allows us to navigate life's uncertainties with grace and determination.

For you, dear reader, resilience is not just an abstract concept; it's a skill you can cultivate in your own life. Whether you're facing a major life challenge or a series of smaller setbacks, know that you have the capacity to bounce back, to adapt, and to grow. Your resilience may not always be apparent in the moment, but with time, you'll see how each challenge has contributed to your strength and ability to keep moving forward.

Resilience is a journey, not a destination. It's about embracing the process of recovery and growth, knowing that every step, no matter how small, is a victory. As you continue on your own path, remember that resilience is within you, ready to be called upon whenever you need it. It's the quiet, persistent force that keeps you going, even when the road is rough, and it's what will carry you through to brighter days ahead.

Self-esteem

Another strength I possess is often described as the foundation of our sense of self-worth, a deep-seated belief in our own value and abilities. For many of us, this belief is hard-won, especially after facing significant challenges and traumas that can shake us to our core. But as I have learned through my own journey, it is possible to rebuild, to rise stronger and more confident than ever before.

In the early stages of my healing, I grappled with self-doubt. Having faced a serious health crisis, I questioned everything about myself, my abilities, my future, and even my worth. The physical and emotional scars were a constant reminder of the battles I had fought. At that time, the idea of stepping in front of a camera, let alone doing anything bold or public, seemed like a distant dream.

But life has a way of surprising us when we least expect it. A few months after my surgery, an opportunity came my way that I never imagined I would have the courage to seize. I was invited to walk the runway, modelling African clothes during International Women's Day. It was more than a fashion show; it was a celebration of resilience, culture, and the strength of women. Standing on that stage, wearing the vibrant fabrics that spoke of my heritage and my journey, I felt a surge of confidence I hadn't felt in a long time. It was as if the act of walking that runway was symbolic of my path to recovery, a bold step forward, a reclaiming of my self-worth.

That first step opened doors I hadn't even known were there. Soon after, I found myself appearing on billboards and social platforms as a commercial model in the Republic of Ireland and Northern Ireland. I was featured in major brands, including Heineken, Dalata Hotel Group, Tourism Northern Ireland, AIB Bank, Aer Lingus, and the Dublin Electoral Commission. Imagine my surprise when I saw my own image on Dublin buses, a city I had come to call home. It was a surreal experience, but also a powerful affirmation that I was more than my trauma; I was a symbol of survival and strength.

But the journey didn't stop there. With each success, my confidence grew. I began to realise that surviving what I had been through didn't just mean enduring pain; it meant being refined, shaped into someone stronger, more resilient, and more capable. My experiences had given me a unique voice, and I soon found myself stepping into yet another arena I had once doubted I belonged in: public speaking.

Public speaking is often cited as one of the greatest fears people have, but for me, it became a platform for empowerment. I was invited to speak at various events, sharing my story, my insights, and my message of resilience. Each time I took the stage, I felt a connection with the audience, a shared understanding that life's challenges could be met with courage and grace. One of the most memorable highlights of this journey was the incredible honour of being invited to speak on Botswana National Television (BTV) for International Women's Day, despite being miles away in Ireland. Connecting via Skype, I was truly humbled to share my voice on such a meaningful occasion, bridging continents to celebrate and advocate for women everywhere.

It was a full-circle moment, honouring the strength and wisdom of my mother, who had always been my greatest inspiration.

Through all these experiences, I've come to understand that self-esteem isn't about being perfect or never doubting yourself. It's about recognising your worth, even in the face of adversity, and having the courage to step into your potential. The journey to self-esteem is often a winding road, marked by both setbacks and triumphs, but it is one worth travelling.

If you take anything away from my story, let it be this: If I survived what did not kill me, it was only refining me into the woman I am today, and the woman I am still becoming. Every scar, every struggle, every moment of doubt, was part of the process that brought me here, standing confidently in my abilities and my worth. And you, too, can find that strength within yourself. It's there, waiting to be discovered, refined, and embraced.

Emotional Regulation

Mastering emotional regulation is another profound gift that growth from trauma has given me; it has allowed me to regulate my emotions more effectively. Emotional regulation is about learning to respond to emotions in a healthy, balanced way rather than being controlled by them. It's a skill that I've had to cultivate over time, especially after the challenges I've faced, and it's one that has transformed how I navigate the ups and downs of life.

In the past, I found myself easily irritated or upset by minor inconveniences or thoughtless comments. Little things that didn't go as planned could throw off my entire day, leaving me drained and frustrated. But as I healed and grew from my traumatic experiences, I began to see how much energy I was wasting on things that didn't truly matter.

This growth allowed me to step back and ask myself, "Is this worth my peace?" More often than not, the answer was no. I learned to protect my energy and prioritise my well-being, choosing not to let the trivialities of life disrupt my inner calm. Now, when something minor happens that might have once annoyed me – like someone cutting me off in traffic or a delayed appointment – I remind myself that these are small moments in the grand scheme of things. They don't deserve the power to derail my peace.

Emotional regulation also means acknowledging and honouring my feelings without letting them dictate my actions. It's not about suppressing emotions or pretending everything is fine when it's not. Instead, it's about recognising emotions as they arise, understanding their source, and responding thoughtfully rather than reactively. For example, when I feel anger or frustration bubbling up, I take a moment to breathe, reflect, and choose a response that aligns with my values and goals, rather than simply reacting on impulse.

It is worth noting that emotional regulation is a skill that can be developed over time. It's about creating a buffer between the emotion and the response, giving yourself the space to choose how you want to handle the situation. This doesn't mean that emotions won't affect you – they're a natural part of being human – but it does mean that you have the power to decide how much control they have over your actions and your day.

Protecting your energy and peace is essential for emotional well-being. By learning to regulate your emotions, you can conserve your energy for the things that truly matter, rather than letting it be drained by every annoyance or frustration that comes your way. Over time, you'll find that this practice not only reduces stress but also enhances your overall sense of happiness and contentment.

Remember, emotional regulation is not about perfection. There will be moments when emotions get the best of us, and that's okay. What's important is the overall trend, the gradual shift towards greater control over your emotional responses. It's a journey of growth, and each step you take towards mastering your emotions is a step towards a more peaceful and fulfilling life.

Optimism

On my journey of post-traumatic growth (PTG), one essential item I couldn't leave out of my bag is optimism. After everything I've been through, I have a deep sense of hope and a positive outlook on life and its future possibilities. This optimism isn't about thinking positively for the sake of it; it's about believing in the potential for good things to come, even when life has shown you its toughest moments.

Optimism has been a guiding light for me, especially during the darkest times. It's the belief that no matter how challenging things may seem, there's always a way forward, always something to look forward to. This mindset didn't come easily. It was something I had to work on, especially after facing significant trauma. But through healing and growth, I learned that optimism is not simply a feeling; it's a choice. It's a conscious decision to focus on what can be, rather than being consumed by what was.

I want to share that optimism is a powerful tool you can carry with you as well. It's like a compass that points you towards possibilities, guiding you through the uncertainty of life. When you choose to be optimistic, you're choosing to see opportunities where others might see obstacles. You're deciding to believe in a future that holds promise, even if the present feels overwhelming. I'm hopeful not just for myself, but for everyone who reads this book. I truly believe that my story, this story of resilience, growth, and transformation, has the potential to touch lives across the globe. My experiences, though deeply personal, are shared with you in the hope that they will inspire and empower. I want you to see that no matter what you've been through, there is always a path forward, and there are always reasons to be hopeful.

Optimism is about looking ahead with faith in what's to come. It's about knowing that your past doesn't define your future and that every day is an opportunity to create a new chapter in your life. As you read through these pages, I hope you feel that same sense of hope – hope for your own life, for the challenges you might be facing, and for the incredible possibilities that lie ahead. This journey we're on, this path of growth and discovery, is filled with opportunities for optimism. So, as you continue reading, I invite you to embrace this mindset. Let my story be a reminder that no matter where you are right now, there's always a reason to believe in a brighter tomorrow. Together, let's keep that hope alive, and let's carry it forward as we each navigate our own paths, filled with optimism for the future.

The Gift of Empathy

In the aftermath of challenging situations, one of the most profound changes I've experienced is the deepening of my empathy. When you've been through something difficult, you gain a unique understanding of pain, struggle, and resilience. You come to realise how fragile life can be, and with that realisation comes a heightened sensitivity to the experiences of others. This is why empathy is such an essential part of my post-traumatic growth (PTG) journey. It's a powerful gift that allows me to connect with others on a deeper level.

Empathy isn't only about feeling sorry for someone else's struggles; it's about truly understanding them. It's the ability to place yourself in someone else's shoes, to see the world from their perspective, and to feel their emotions as if they were your own. After surviving my own battles, I found that I could relate to others' pain in a way I never could before. I could offer comfort, not only because I wanted to, but because I genuinely understood what they were going through.

This empathy has transformed how I interact with people. It has made me more compassionate, more patient, and more willing to listen. When someone shares their struggles with me, I don't only hear their words; I feel their pain, their fear, their hope. This connection allows me to offer support that is not just kind, but meaningful. It's the kind of support that says, "I've been there, and I'm here for you." I want to highlight how empathy can be a source of strength and connection in your own life. When you've faced challenges, you gain a perspective that many others may not have. This perspective enables you to reach out to others with genuine understanding, creating bonds that are based on shared human experiences. Your empathy becomes a bridge, a way to connect with others who might be feeling isolated in their own struggles.

Imagine a world where we all carry this kind of empathy in our hearts. A world where, instead of judging or dismissing others, we take the time to understand their journey. This kind of empathy can transform relationships, heal wounds, and foster a sense of community that is desperately needed in today's world.

As you continue your own journey of growth, I encourage you to embrace the empathy that comes from your experiences. Let it guide your interactions with others and allow it to deepen your connections. Your empathy is not only a reminder of what you've been through; it's a powerful tool that can help others heal, as you have healed. Through empathy, we create a ripple effect of understanding and compassion that can change the world, one interaction at a time.

So, as you carry your own bag of post-traumatic growth, remember to cherish the empathy it contains. Use it to make the world a little kinder, a little more connected, and a lot more understanding. Your empathy is a gift, one that not only helps others but also enriches your own life in ways you may never have imagined.

Social Support

Social support emerges as one of the most vital strengths. Positive relationships are crucial not only for your growth and well-being but also for navigating the complexities of life after trauma. Through my experiences, I've come to realise how important it is to surround yourself with people who uplift, support, and encourage you. These are the relationships that align with your values, create positive energy, and help you flourish.

However, it's not simply about having relationships; it's about having the *right* relationships. During my healing process, I became acutely aware of the difference between toxic relationships and effective ones. Toxic relationships drain your energy, undermine your self-worth, and often leave you feeling worse than before. In contrast, effective relationships are those that build you up, offer genuine support, and align with the person you are becoming.

One of the most important lessons I've learned is the power of setting boundaries. Even as I was writing this book, I had to consciously create boundaries with friends, family, and others in my life. This wasn't easy, but it was necessary. I learned to say

"No" more often than I said "Yes" because I understood that my time and energy are precious. Not everyone who enters your life is meant to stay, and not every relationship is worth nurturing.

It's important to be mindful of the people you allow into your inner circle. Beware of time-wasters, those who don't respect your time, your boundaries, or your goals. These individuals can impede your progress and pull you away from the positive path you're on. Instead, focus on cultivating relationships that are effective, those that add value to your life and support your growth.

Your Turn

Think about the relationships in your own life.

Are they nourishing your spirit, or are they draining you? Do they align with your values and contribute to your well-being?

If not, it might be time to reassess and make changes. Remember, you have the right to protect your energy and to surround yourself with people who genuinely care about your growth.

In building this network of positive relationships, you create a support system that not only helps you through tough times but also celebrates with you in your victories. These are the people who will stand by you, encourage you, and help you become the best version of yourself. They are a crucial part of your PTG journey, and their support can make all the difference.

As you move forward, I encourage you to be intentional about the relationships you foster. Seek out those who lift you up, who share your values, and who inspire you to keep growing. And don't be afraid to let go of those who don't. Your well-being depends on it, and your journey towards growth and healing will be all the stronger for it.

In conclusion, post-traumatic growth (PTG) is a transformative process where individuals emerge stronger, more resilient, and more purpose-driven after experiencing trauma. It's not just about surviving difficult times but about thriving in the aftermath, discovering new strengths, and gaining a deeper understanding of life.

The benefits of PTG are profound. It can lead to an enhanced appreciation of life, deeper connections with others, and a renewed sense of purpose. When experiencing PTG you might often find yourselves more empathetic, resilient, and optimistic. You develop a stronger sense of self-worth, and become more confident in your abilities, and better able to regulate your emotions. In essence, PTG **turns adversity into an opportunity for personal growth and fulfilment**.

In the workplace, the principles of PTG can be incredibly beneficial. By embracing the lessons learned from past challenges, you can bring a unique perspective to your professional life. You'll likely find yourself more adaptable, better equipped to handle stress, and more creative in problem-solving. These qualities are invaluable in achieving success and fostering positive relationships in any professional setting.

Moreover, the importance of finding a coach who understands PTG, like myself, cannot be overstated. As a coach, my role is to guide you through the process of recognising and harnessing the growth that comes from trauma, helping you to apply these insights in your personal and professional life. With the right support, you can turn your struggles into stepping stones towards a more fulfilling and successful future.

PTG is not simply about overcoming trauma; it's about embracing the growth that comes from it. By understanding and applying the principles of PTG, you can unlock new levels of resilience, creativity, and success in your life and career. And with the right guidance, you can navigate this journey with confidence, transforming adversity into a powerful catalyst for growth and achievement.

....

PEARLS OF WISDOM

Growth Through Adversity

True abundance often emerges from the most difficult experiences. Pain and trauma can serve as powerful catalysts for personal growth, transforming our mindset and strengthening our resilience.

Shifting Perspectives

Abundance isn't solely about material wealth; it's a state of mind. When we shift our focus from scarcity to gratitude, even the smallest blessings can create a sense of richness in our lives.

Healing Requires Time and Patience

Post-traumatic growth doesn't happen overnight. It takes patience, self-compassion, and the willingness to confront uncomfortable emotions to heal and grow from trauma.

Gratitude is the Foundation of Abundance

Practicing gratitude allows us to recognise the positive in every situation. By focusing on what we have, rather than what we lack, we can cultivate an abundant mindset even in times of hardship.

Resilience Is a Skill

The ability to bounce back from trauma or hardship is not an inherent trait, but a skill that can be developed. Every setback is an opportunity to build your emotional strength and resilience.

Abundance Comes From Within

While external success may fluctuate, true abundance is internal. It's the peace, joy, and fulfilment we feel regardless of our circumstances.

Post-Traumatic Growth Redefines Success

After experiencing trauma, many people redefine their understanding of success. It becomes less about outward achievements and more about emotional growth, deeper connections, and inner peace.

Helping Others Heals Ourselves

Sharing your journey of overcoming trauma can inspire and uplift others. In supporting others, you reinforce your own healing and strengthen the sense of abundance in your life.

Self-Belief Is Essential

Believing in your ability to grow from trauma is key to post-traumatic growth. When you trust in your strength, you open the door to profound transformation and the discovery of abundance in unexpected places.

The Power of Perspective

Trauma may change our life's course, but it doesn't have to limit us. By embracing the lessons it teaches and shifting our perspective, we can not only survive but thrive, experiencing life in a fuller, more abundant way.

APPENDICES

REFERENCES

Part 1: Letting Go

[1] Hunt, A. (2020, August 10). *Two Monks and a Woman.* Alpha Home. https://www.alphahome.org/two-monks-and-a-woman/

[2] Diamond, J., *My Distant Dad: Healing the Father Wound.* Lasting Impact Press, 2018

[3] Purkiss, J., *The Power of Letting Go: How to drop everything that's holding you back.* Aster, 2020

[4] Fear. (2024, September 4). *Cambridge Dictionary.* https://dictionary.cambridge.org/dictionary/english/fear

[5] Gottberg, K. (2017, March 31). The Ho'oponopono Power of Forgiveness and Letting Go, SMART Living 365. https://www.smartliving365.com/the-hooponopono-power-of-forgiveness-and-letting-go/

[6] Mind Body Soul (Director). (2022, October 7). Ho'oponopono Prayer, 108 Repetitions For Deep Healing & Forgiveness, Powerful Mantra Meditation [Video recording].YouTube. https://www.youtube.com/watch?v=lNeiLi882MU

[7] Dweck, Carol, *Mindset: The New Psychology of Success*, Random House, 2006

Part 2: Keep On Keeping On

[8] *Keep on doing something*. (2024, October 23). *Cambridge Dictionary*. https://dictionary.cambridge.org/dictionary/english/keep-on-doing

[9] Bob Dylan: *Tangled Up In Blue* | The Official Bob Dylan Site. (n.d.). Retrieved 5 October 2024, from https://www.bobdylan.com/songs/tangled-blue/

[10] Sharma, Robin, *The Monk Who Sold His Ferrari*, Harper Thorsons, 2015

[11] Hay, Louise, *You Can Heal Your Life*, Hay House, 1984

[12] Singer, Michael A., *The Untethered Soul*, New Harbinger, 2007

[13] Brown, Brené, *Daring Greatly: How the Courage to Be Vulnerable Transforms the Way We Live, Love, Parent, and Lead*, Penguin Life, 2015

[14] The Dalai Lama and Cutler, Howard, *The Art of Happiness: A Handbook for Living*, Hodder Paperbacks, 1999

[15] Kabat-Zinn, Jon, *Wherever You Go, There You Are: Mindfulness meditation for everyday life*, Piatkus, 2004

Part 3: Hope

[16] Unknown. (n.d.). *Story Of A Poor Farmer* | BULB. Retrieved 9 April 2024, from https://www.bulbapp.io/p/d93b8925-f937-48cb-bca8-816d93c32ff0/story-of-a-poor-farmer

[17] Hoyt, C. L., Burnette, J. L., Nash, E., Becker, W., & Billingsley, J. (2023). Growth mindsets of anxiety: Do the benefits to individual

flourishing come with societal costs? *The Journal of Positive Psychology*, 18(3), 370–382. https://doi.org/10.1080/17439760.2021.2006762

[18] Oprah Reflects on the Act of Kindness That Changed Her Life: "I'll Take It to My Grave". (2019, July 10). *Oprah Daily*. https://www.oprahdaily.com/life/a28321896/oprah-beef-trial-act-of-kindness/

Part 4: Grief

[19] Mughal, S., Azhar, Y., Mahon, M. M., & Siddiqui, W. J. (2024). *Grief Reaction and Prolonged Grief Disorder*. StatPearls Publishing. http://www.ncbi.nlm.nih.gov/books/NBK507832/

[20] Kübler-Ross, E., *On Death and Dying: What the Dying Have to Teach Doctors, Nurses, Clergy, and Their Own Family*. Macmillan, 1970

[21] Gaffney, M., *Flourishing: How to achieve a deeper sense of well-being, meaning and purpose – even when facing adversity*, Penguin Life, 2015

[22] Grief. (n.d.). American Psychological Association. Retrieved October 27, 2024, from https://www.apa.org/topics/grief

[23] Mind in View. (n.d.). Starting from *Grief Pt. 1* [Audio podcast episode]. Apple Podcasts. Retrieved October 27, 2024, from https://podcasts.apple.com/us/podcast/mind-in-view/id1544156706

[24] Coleman, P., *Finding Peace When Your Heart Is in Pieces: A Step-by-Step Guide to the Other Side of Grief, Loss, and Pain*, Adams Media, 2014

[25] How to overcome grief's health-damaging effects. (2018, April 1). *Harvard Health*. https://www.health.harvard.edu/mind-and-mood/how-to-overcome-griefs-health-damaging-effects

[26] Bui, E., Chad-Friedman, E., Wieman, S., Grasfield, R. H., Rolfe, A., Dong, M., Park, E. R., & Denninger, J. W. (2018). Patient and Provider Perspectives on a Mind-Body Program for Grieving Older Adults. *The American Journal of Hospice & Palliative Care*, 35(6), 858–865. https://doi.org/10.1177/1049909117743956

[27] Macfarlane, J. (2020). Positive psychology: Social connectivity and its role within mental health nursing. *British Journal of Mental Health Nursing*, 9(2), 1–12. https://doi.org/10.12968/bjmh.2020.0007

[28] Are Some Social Ties Better Than Others? (n.d.). *Greater Good*. Retrieved 28 October 2024, from https://greatergood.berkeley.edu/article/item/are_some_ties_better_than_others

[29] Yeung, A., Chan, J. S. M., Cheung, J. C., & Zou, L. (2018). Qigong and Tai-Chi for Mood Regulation. *FOCUS*, 16(1), 40–47. https://doi.org/10.1176/appi.focus.20170042

[30] Szuhany, K. L., Malgaroli, M., Miron, C. D., & Simon, N. M. (2021). Prolonged Grief Disorder: Course, Diagnosis, Assessment, and Treatment. Focus: *Journal of Life Long Learning in Psychiatry*, 19(2), 161–172. https://doi.org/10.1176/appi.focus.20200052

[31] Neff, K. (n.d.). *Self-compassion*. Retrieved September 4, 2024, from https://self-compassion.org/

[32] Johnson, E., & O'Brien, K. (2013), Self-Compassion Soothes the Savage EGO-Threat System: Effects on Negative Affect, Shame, Rumination, and Depressive Symptoms. *Journal of Social and Clinical Psychology*, 32(9), 939–963.

[33] Neff, K. D., & Germer, C. K. (2013). A pilot study and randomized controlled trial of the mindful self-compassion program. *Journal of Clinical Psychology*, 69(1), 28–44. https://doi.org/10.1002/jclp.21923

[34] Behan, C. (2020). The benefits of meditation and mindfulness practices during times of crisis such as COVID-19. *Irish Journal of Psychological Medicine*, 37(1), 1–3. https://doi.org/10.1017/ipm.2020.38

[35] Sharma, H. (2015). Meditation: Process and effects. *Ayu*, 36(3), 233–237. https://doi.org/10.4103/0974-8520.182756

[36] Stephenson, J. (Director). (2014, October 21). Coping with grief: Guided spoken meditation for healing after a loss of a loved one [Video recording]. YouTube. https://www.youtube.com/watch?v=qB6KKQRQzXs

Part 5: Patience and Perseverance

[37] The Power of Patience: How to Wait Well, Persevere Through Suffering, and Navigate a Fast-Paced World with Dr. Sarah Schnitker. (n.d.). *Thrive Center.* Retrieved 29 October 2024, from https://thethrivecenter.org/episodes/the-power-of-patience-how-to-wait-well-persevere-through-suffering-and-navigate-a-fast-paced-world-with-dr-sarah-schnitker/

[38] Schnitker, S. A. (2012). An examination of patience and well-being. *The Journal of Positive Psychology*, 7(4), 263–280. https://doi.org/10.1080/17439760.2012.697185

[39] Al-Arja, N. S. (2023). Patience and its relationship to stress tolerance in relation to demographic factors of the medical system in Bethlehem Governorate during the COVID-19 pandemic. *Frontiers in Psychology*, 14, 1059589. https://doi.org/10.3389/fpsyg.2023.1059589

[40] Schnitker, S., & Emmons, R. (2007). Patience as a virtue: Religious and psychological perspectives (pp. 177–207). https://doi.org/10.1163/ej.9789004158511.i-301.69

[41] Wood, A. M., Froh, J. J., & Geraghty, A. W. A. (2010). Gratitude and well-being: A review and theoretical integration. *Clinical Psychology Review*, 30(7), 890–905. https://doi.org/10.1016/j.cpr.2010.03.005

[42] Datu, J. A. D. (2021). Beyond Passion and Perseverance: Review and Future Research Initiatives on the Science of Grit. *Frontiers in Psychology*, 11, 545526. https://doi.org/10.3389/fpsyg.2020.545526

[43] Duckworth, A. L., Peterson, C., Matthews, M. D., & Kelly, D. R. (2007). Grit: Perseverance and passion for long-term goals. *Journal of Personality and Social Psychology*, 92(6), 1087–1101. https://doi.org/10.1037/0022-3514.92.6.1087

[44] Seligman, Martin, *Learned Optimism: How to Change Your Mind and Your Life*, Knopf Doubleday Publishing Group, 1990

[45] Self-efficacy: Bandura's theory of motivation in psychology. (2023, July 10). *Simply Psychology*. https://www.simplypsychology.org/self-efficacy.html

[46] Helen Steiner Rice Thinking of You Picturesque Scenery Nice Verse New Card. (n.d.). *Occasion Cards*. Retrieved February 23, 2024, from https://www.occasioncards.co.uk/helen-steiner-rice-thinking-of-you-picturesque-scenery-nice-verse-new-card/

[47] The Royal Melbourne Hospital. (n.d.). Breast reconstruction using DIEP flap. https://thewomens.r.worldssl.net/images/uploads/fact-sheets/Breast-reconstruction-using-DIEP-flap-160119.pdf

[48] Coelho, Paulo, *The Alchemist*, HarperCollins, 2012

Part 6: Self-Belief

[49] Self-Belief definition and meaning, *Collins English Dictionary*. Retrieved 21 February 2024, https://www.collinsdictionary.com/dictionary/english/self-belief

[50] Creswell, J. D., Dutcher, J. M., Klein, W. M. P., Harris, P. R., & Levine, J. M. (2013). Self-Affirmation Improves Problem-Solving under Stress. *PLoS ONE*, 8(5), e62593. https://doi.org/10.1371/journal.pone.0062593

Part 7: Radiance of Positive Self-Talk

[51] Radiance. (2024, October 23). *Collins Dictionary*. https://dictionary.cambridge.org/dictionary/english/radiance

[52] Positive self-talk: Benefits, examples, and tips. (2022, March 18). *Medical News Today*. https://www.medicalnewstoday.com/articles/positive-self-talk

[53] Shadinger, D., Katsion, J., Myllykangas, S., & Case, D. (2019). The Impact of a Positive, Self-Talk Statement on Public Speaking Anxiety. *College Teaching*, 68(1), 5–11. https://doi.org/10.1080/87567555.2019.1680522

[54] Sadri Damirchi, E., Mojarrad, A., Pireinaladin, S., & Grjibovski, A. M. (2020). The Role of Self-Talk in Predicting Death Anxiety, Obsessive-Compulsive Disorder, and Coping Strategies in the Face of Coronavirus Disease (COVID-19). *Iranian Journal of Psychiatry*, 15(3), 182–188. https://doi.org/10.18502/ijps.v15i3.3810

[55] Muccino, G. (Director). (2006). *The Pursuit of Happyness* [Film]. Columbia Pictures. Based on the true story of Chris Gardner, starring Will Smith.

Part 8: Visualisation

[56] Visualization. (2024, October 23). *Cambridge Dictionary*. https://dictionary.cambridge.org/dictionary/english/visualization

[57] Farrelly, P. (Director). (1994). *Dumb and Dumber* [Film]. New Line Cinema.

[58] 8 Successful People Who Use The Power Of Visualization. (2015, July 8). *Mindbodygreen*. https://www.mindbodygreen.com/articles/successful-people-who-use-the-power-of-visualization

[59] Bolton, M. (1990). *When I'm back on my feet again* [Song]. On *Soul Provider* [Album]. Columbia Records. https://www.youtube.com/watch?v=ALU23yoRPm4

[60] Ranganathan, V. K., Siemionow, V., Liu, J. Z., Sahgal, V., & Yue, G. H. (2004). From mental power to muscle power: gaining strength by using the mind. *Neuropsychologia*, 42(7), 944–956.

[61] Gundan, F. (n.d.). Dr. Myles Munroe: On Leadership, Vision, Purpose And Maximizing Your Potential. *Forbes*. Retrieved 26 October 2024, from https://www.forbes.com/sites/faraigundan/2014/11/10/dr-myles-munroe-on-leadership-vision-purpose-and-maximizing-your-potential/

[62] The Mindful Movement (Director). (2021, June 22). Design your Dream Life: A Guided Visualization and Meditation. *Mindful Movement* [Video recording]. https://www.youtube.com/watch?v=ziOryqljzf4

Part Nine: Embracing Abundance "Letlotlo"

[63] Perissos Meaning, Greek Lexicon | New Testament (NAS). (n.d.). *Bible Study Tools*. Retrieved 26 October 2024, from https://www.biblestudytools.com/lexicons/greek/nas/perissos.html

[64] Abundance definition and meaning. *Cambridge Dictionary*. https://dictionary.cambridge.org/dictionary/english/abundance#google_vignette

[65] Greater Good Science Center. (n.d.). The Science of Gratitude. University of California, Berkeley. https://ggsc.berkeley.edu/images/uploads/GGSC-JTF_White_Paper-Gratitude-FINAL.pdf

[66] Seligman, M, *Flourish*, Simon and Schuster Audio, 2011

[67] Csikszentmihalyi, M., *Flow: The Psychology of Optimal Experience*, HarperCollins, 1990

[68] *Trauma*. (n.d.). American Psychological Association. Retrieved July 23, 2024, from https://www.apa.org/topics/trauma

[69] Tedeschi, R.G., & Moore, B. A. *The Post-Traumatic Growth Workbook: Coming Through Trauma Wiser, Stronger, and More Resilient*, Kogan Page, 2020

[70] Burke, J., Dune, P. J., Meehan, T., O'Boyle, C. A., van Nieuwerburgh, C. *Positive Health: 100+ Research-based Positive Psychology and Lifestyle Medicine Tools to Enhance Your Wellbeing*. Routledge, Taylor & Francis Group, 2023

[71] Boniwell, I., & Tunariu, A. D. *Positive Psychology: Theory, Research and Applications*, McGraw-Hill Education, 2019

[72] Tedeschi R.G, Calhoun L.G. The post-traumatic growth inventory: Measuring the positive legacy of trauma. *Journal of Trauma & Stress*, 9(3), 455–471. https://doi.org/10.1007/BF02103658

[73] Tony Robbins, *Where focus goes, energy flows* [Video]. (2016, March 22). YouTube. https://www.youtube.com/watch?v=b8jS86OtgLA

[74] Gordon, D. D., *Charge Yourself Up for Success Energizing Your Life, Work and Relationships*, Beyond Publishing, 2023

WEBSITES AND JOURNALS

APA Dictionary of Psychology. (n.d.). *APA Dictionary of Psychology*. Retrieved April 9, 2024, from https://dictionary.apa.org/

Self-talk. (2022, March 4). Healthdirect Australia. https://www.healthdirect.gov.au/self-talk

Howells, Kerry, (2020, June 22). *How can we find gratitude in the midst of grief?* Kerry Howells. https://kerryhowells.com/how-can-we-find-gratitude-in-the-midst-of-grief/

Ali, Massa Mohamed, HBSc Candidate, University of Toronto, (n.d.). The Science of Visualization: Can Imagining Your Goals Make You More Likely To Accomplish Them? *Neurovine.* Retrieved May 17, 2024, from https://www.neurovine.ai/blog/the-science-of-visualization-can-imagining-your-goals-make-you-more-likely-to-accomplish-them

Big Knows, (2022, May 30). *Visualise, Visualise, Visualise – Your Ultimate Mental Weapon*. Big Knows. https://big-knows.co.uk/visualise-visualise-visualise-your-ultimate-mental-weapon/

Evaggelidou, Sophia. (2023, September 25). 5 Tips to Build Unwavering Self-Belief: And Why It Matters. Mindvalley Blog. https://blog.mindvalley.com/self-belief/

Bartolomei-Torres, Pierette, (2024, March 11). Albert Bandura's Efficacy Theory: How Self-Belief Impacts Personal Success. *Learningbp*. https://www.learningbp.com/albert-banduras-efficacy-theory-how-self-belief-impacts-personal-success/

Leeman. (n.d.). Clinical practice review on post-traumatic growth among healthcare professionals post COVID-19 and the facilitation of health outcomes for the patient and client population group. *Journal of Hospital Management and Health Policy*. Retrieved September 27, 2024, from https://jhmhp.amegroups.org/article/view/8441/html

Lee, C., Park, S., & Jang, H. (2018). Double mediating effects of growth mindset and hope between tourism experience and psychological Well-Being. *Indian Journal of Public Health Research & Development*, 9, 1221. https://doi.org/10.5958/0976-5506.2018.01162.2

Predko, V. (2021). Effect of Covid-19 on hardiness. In *Mental health, well-being & loneliness during COVID-19*. Retrieved from https://www.academia.edu/58617460/EFFECT_OF_COVID_19_ON_HARDINESS

nat-zen_com. (2022, September 13). Examples of positive self-talk. *Nat-Zen*. https://nat-zen.com/examples-of-positive-self-talk/

Peterson, S., & Byron, K. (2008). Exploring the role of hope in job performance: Results from four studies. *Journal of Organizational Behavior*, 29, 785–803. https://doi.org/10.1002/job.492

Five famous (and several not-so-famous) grief quotes. (2021, March 24). Marie Curie. https://www.mariecurie.org.uk/talkabout/articles/famous-quotes-about-grief/268300

Grief meditation: How to use mindfulness to heal after loss. (n.d.). Calm Blog. Retrieved 28 September 2024, from https://blog.calm.com/blog/grief-meditation

John Quincy Adams Quotes. (n.d.). BrainyQuote. Retrieved 23 February 2024, from https://www.brainyquote.com/quotes/john_quincy_adams_387094

Conversano, C., Rotondo, A., Lensi, E., Della Vista, O., Arpone, F., & Reda, M. A. (2010). Optimism and Its Impact on Mental and Physical Well-Being. *Clinical Practice and Epidemiology in Mental Health* : CP & EMH, 6, 25–29. https://doi.org/10.2174/1745017901006010025

Roques, Anne, (2023, April 30). Post-traumatic growth. Coaching at Work. https://www.coaching-at-work.com/2023/04/30/post-traumatic-growth/

Rodgers, S. T. (2014). Post-traumatic Growth. *Encyclopaedia of Social Work.* https://doi.org/10.1093/acrefore/9780199975839.013.1001

Roepke, A. M. (2015). Psychosocial interventions and post-traumatic growth: A meta-analysis. *Journal of Consulting and Clinical Psychology*, 83(1), 129–142. https://doi.org/10.1037/a0036872

CPPA Students, (2021, July 7). Self-Compassion | Positive Psychology Concepts Series. Medium. https://cppastudents.medium.com/self-compassion-positive-psychology-concepts-series-8b040b82a6e

Speaking Grief | Understanding Grief: There is no step-by-step process. (n.d.). Retrieved 26 August 2024, from https://speakinggrief.org/get-better-at-grief/understanding-grief/no-step-by-step-process

Weir, Kirsten, The gritty truth. (n.d.). American Psychological Association. Retrieved August 24, 2024, from https://www.apa.org/news/apa/2020/gritty-truth

The Health Coach Institute. (2022, May 24). The History of Health Coaching. Holistic Health and Wellness Training. https://www.healthcoachinstitute.com/articles/history-of-health-coaching/

The Psychology of Patience | Hogan Assessments. (n.d.). Retrieved 27 September 2024, from https://www.hoganassessments.com/blog/psychology-patience-personality/

Transformation after trauma, with Richard Tedeschi, PhD. (n.d.). American Psychological Association. Retrieved September 27, 2024, from https://www.apa.org/news/podcasts/speaking-of-psychology/transformation-trauma

Understanding the five stages of grief. (n.d.). Cruse Bereavement Support. Retrieved 27 February 2024, from https://www.cruse.org.uk/understanding-grief/effects-of-grief/five-stages-of-grief/

What Is the Bargaining Stage of Grief? (2022, August 22). Oprah Daily. https://www.oprahdaily.com/life/health/a40943027/understanding-bargaining-stage-of-grief/

Huckerby, D. (2020, May 22). Why Kindness is an Essential Ingredient for Care. Crouched Friars. https://www.crouchedfriars.co.uk/why-kindness-is-an-essential-ingredient-for-care/

Frattini, C., (2022, January 31). 12 science-based benefits of meditation. Hunimed. https://www.hunimed.eu/news/12-science-based-benefits-of-meditation/

Collins, Karen (2022, May 17). Can Food Be Thy Medicine? American Institute for Cancer Research. https://www.aicr.org/resources/blog/can-food-be-thy-medicine/

Baník, G., Dědová, M., & Vargová, L. (2022). Cancer-related post-traumatic growth and post-traumatic stress: How are they connected and what are their correlates? *Supportive Care in Cancer: Official Journal of the Multinational Association of Supportive Care in*

Cancer, 30(10), 8183–8192. https://doi.org/10.1007/s00520-022-07252-7

Jones, A. C., Hilton, R., Blair Ely, Gororo, L., Danesh, V., Sevin, C. M., Jackson, J. C., & Boehm, L. M. (2020). Facilitating Post-Traumatic Growth After Critical Illness. *American Journal of Critical Care : An Official Publication, American Association of Critical-Care Nurses*, 29(6), e108–e115. https://doi.org/10.4037/ajcc2020149

Dell'Osso, L., Lorenzi, P., Nardi, B., Carmassi, C., & Carpita, B. (n.d.). Post Traumatic Growth (PTG) in the Frame of Traumatic Experiences. *Clinical Neuropsychiatry*, 19(6), 390–393. https://doi.org/10.36131/cnfioritieditore20220606

Tao, W., Zhao, D., Yue, H., Horton, I., Tian, X., Xu, Z., & Sun, H.-J. (2022). The Influence of Growth Mindset on the Mental Health and Life Events of College Students. *Frontiers in Psychology*, 13, 821206. https://doi.org/10.3389/fpsyg.2022.821206

Fredrickson, B. L. (2001). The Role of Positive Emotions in Positive Psychology. *The American Psychologist*, 56(3), 218–226.

The Importance of Good Quality Sleep. British Society of Lifestyle Medicine. (n.d.). Retrieved 4 October 2024, from https://bslm.org.uk/the-importance-of-good-quality-sleep/

Captari, L. E., Riggs, S. A., & Stephen, K. (2021). Attachment processes following traumatic loss: A mediation model examining identity distress, shattered assumptions, prolonged grief, and posttraumatic growth. *Psychological Trauma: Theory, Research, Practice, and Policy*, 13(1), 94–103. https://doi.org/10.1037/tra0000555

Lahav, Y., Bellin, E. S., & Solomon, Z. (2016). Posttraumatic Growth and Shattered World Assumptions Among Ex-POWs: The Role of Dissociation. *Psychiatry*, 79(4), 418–432. https://doi.org/10.1080/00332747.2016.1142776

Food and Mood Centre, (2019, January 7), https://foodandmoodcentre.com.au/

Godman, Heidi. (2021, September 1). How many fruits and vegetables do we really need? *Harvard Health*. https://www.health.harvard.edu/nutrition/how-many-fruits-and-vegetables-do-we-really-need

LeWine, Howard, E, How much water should I drink a day? (2016, September 6). *Harvard Health*. https://www.health.harvard.edu/staying-healthy/how-much-water-should-you-drink

Nutrition. (n.d.). *Harvard Health*. Retrieved 15 May 2024, from https://www.health.harvard.edu/topics/nutrition

Phillips, E. M., Frates, E. P., & Park, D. J. (2020). Lifestyle Medicine. *Physical Medicine and Rehabilitation Clinics of North America*, 31(4), 515–526. https://doi.org/10.1016/j.pmr.2020.07.006

Rippe, J. M. (2018). Lifestyle Medicine: The Health Promoting Power of Daily Habits and Practices. *American Journal of Lifestyle Medicine*, 12(6), 499–512. https://doi.org/10.1177/1559827618785554

Ryan, R. M., & Deci, E. L. (2000). Self-Determination Theory and the Facilitation of Intrinsic Motivation, Social Development, and Well-Being. *American Psychologist*.

FURTHER READING

Brennan, Dr Sabina, *The Neuroscience of Manifesting: The Magical Science of Getting the Life You Want*, Orion Spring, 2024

Brown, Brené, *Dare to Lead: Brave Work. Tough Conversations. Whole Hearts*, Vermilion, 2018

Covey, Stephen, *The 7 Habits of Highly Effective People: Powerful Lessons in Personal Change*, Simon & Schuster, 2013

Falvey, Pat, *You Have the Power: Explore the Mindset You Need to Realise Your Dreams*, Beyond Endurance Publishing, 2016

Hussey, Gerry, *Awaken Your Power Within: Let Go of Fear. Discover Your Infinite Potential. Become Your True Self.*, Monoray, 2021

Jones, Charlie, *Life is Tremendous: Enthusiasm Makes the Difference!*, Executive Books, 1966

McKenna, Paul, *Change Your Life In 7 Days*, Bantam Press, 2019

McKenna, Paul, *Instant Confidence*, Bantam Press, 2006

Osteen, Joel, *Peaceful on Purpose: The Power to Remain Calm, Strong, and Confident in Every Season*, FaithWords, 2022

Osteen, Joel, *You Are Stronger than You Think: Unleash the Power to Go Bigger, Go Bold, and Go Beyond What Limits You*, FaithWords, 2021

Sagner, Michael, Egger, Gary, Binns, Andrew & Rossner, Stephan, Eds, *Lifestyle Medicine: Lifestyle, the Environment and Preventive Medicine in Health and Disease*, Academic Press, 2017

Sinek, Simon, *Start With Why*, Penguin, 2011

Williams, Mark & Penman, Danny, *Mindfulness: A Practical Guide to Finding Peace in a Frantic World*, Piatkus, 2011

ACKNOWLEDGEMENTS

ONCE THIS BOOK BEGAN transitioning from a concept in my mind to a completed manuscript, many people played a significant role in its journey, and they deserve to be acknowledged and thanked. I would like to express my deepest gratitude to my late mother, who was a powerful role model and taught me the values of love and kindness. To my family and friends, thank you for always believing in me and for encouraging and supporting me through all the challenges I faced before and during the writing of this book.

I would also like to express my deepest gratitude to the publishers of this book, whose expertise, dedication, and unwavering support have been instrumental in bringing this project to life. Their commitment to excellence, from the initial stages of development to the final publication, has been truly inspiring.

A special acknowledgement goes to Brenda Dempsey, who is not only the CEO of Book Brilliance Publishing but also became my mentor, coach, and a true inspiration to me. I am also deeply grateful to Olivia Eisinger, whose sharp editorial eye and thoughtful suggestions helped shape this book into its best possible version. Her professionalism and dedication ensured every word resonated with purpose. Additionally, my thanks go to Zara Thatcher, whose meticulous typesetting and proofreading work brought the pages to life with elegance and clarity.

To all the organisations and individuals who gave me the opportunity to lead, be led by, or observe their leadership from afar, I am profoundly thankful. You have been the inspiration and foundation of my leadership journey. To my teachers and lecturers across the globe, I owe a heartfelt thank you for shaping me into the person I am today.

ABOUT THE AUTHOR

Pearl Letlotlo Olesitse is a dedicated healthcare professional, coach and public speaker with a dynamic career spanning clinical leadership, nursing, and research. Born and raised in Botswana, she brings a unique perspective to her work, drawing from her diverse experiences in national and international healthcare settings. Now based in Dublin, Ireland, she specialises in healthcare and dermatology research, contributing to impactful projects that advance patient care and medical knowledge.

Pearl holds a BSc in Nursing from the University of Botswana, a First-Class Honours in Marketing (Digital Media and Cloud Computing) from Dublin Business School, and a Master of

Science in Positive Health Coaching from the Royal College of Surgeons in Ireland (RCSI), University of Medicine and Health Sciences. Her academic and professional achievements reflect her commitment to excellence, even under challenging circumstances.

An inspiring public speaker, Pearl has appeared on the national and international stage. She is passionate about empowering others to transform their lives through storytelling, leadership, and coaching, positioning her as an authority in the field of leadership transformation.

Pearl enjoys reading and writing, particularly on positive psychology and lifestyle medicine topics. She is committed to both personal and professional growth, with hobbies that include modelling, learning languages, playing the guitar, and chess. Her work drives a strong desire to succeed and to inspire others to achieve their goals.

www.pearllolesitse.com

www.linkedin.com/in/pearl-letlotlo-olesitse-msc-bsc-rgn-ba-hons-cpnlp-3bb9a5107

www.youtube.com/@pearl-letlotlo-olesitse

www.instagram.com/pearll_olesitse/

https://x.com/pearll_olesitse

polesitse@yahoo.com

polesitse@gmail.com

www.ingramcontent.com/pod-product-compliance
Lightning Source LLC
Chambersburg PA
CBHW051714020426
42333CB00014B/990
* 9 7 8 1 9 1 3 7 7 0 9 8 3 *